WORKSHOP 5

by and for teachers

THE WRITING PROCESS REVISITED
edited by
Thomas Newkirk

HEINEMANN
Portsmouth, New Hampshire

Published by
Heinemann
A division of Reed Publishing (USA) Inc.
361 Hanover Street   Portsmouth, NH 03801-3912
Offices and agents throughout the world

Every effort has been made to contact the copyright holders for permission to reprint borrowed material where necessary. We regret any oversights that may have occurred and would be happy to rectify them in future printings of this work.

The publisher is grateful to the following for permission to reprint previously published material:

Page 153: Untitled poem beginning "The last berries . . ." reprinted with permission of Macmillan Publishing Company from *Inside Turtle's Shell and Other Poems of the Field* by Joanne Ryder. Copyright © 1985 by Joanne Ryder.

ISBN 0-435-08798-3
ISSN 1043-1705

Design by Wladislaw Finne

Printed in the United States of America on acid-free paper
97   96   95   94   93   BB   5   4   3   2   1

CONTENTS

ABOUT
WORKSHOP 5

When I interviewed Donald Graves for this issue of *Workshop*, he admitted that he could hardly say the words "writing process." He shook his head, "I just can't get them out of my mouth." Educational terms, after all, have a short half-life. They begin to lose their force almost immediately, assuming so many meanings that they become unrecognizable to those who made them popular. And like someone condemned to watch late night parodies of himself, Don can only wince when he hears people debate the "three-steps Graves" versus the "five-steps Graves" approaches. One of the paradoxes of writing is that it fixes a person's position; Graves has become identified with earlier positions that he himself no longer holds. (He also admitted that he could no longer stand to read his own bestseller, *Writing: Teachers and Children at Work*.)

It seemed to me that we should mark the tenth birthday of Graves' book with a revisiting and rethinking of some of the early writing process work. The issue begins with a wide-ranging interview with Don in which he reflects upon the autobiographical roots of his work, his early writing process research, and the changes in his thinking since then. The portrait that emerges is, I believe, somewhat different from the one many have of him. When I showed the interview to Don Murray, my neighbor and Don's close friend, he wrote the following:

> You captured the Don Graves I know, the Don Graves that asks tough, significant questions; the Don Graves that demands focused, documented answers; the Don Graves that is concerned about learning in a hard headed, Yankee, intellectual way; the Don Graves who

takes risks and is accountable, willing to evaluate his work almost ruthlessly and without apology; the Don Graves whose romanticism is balanced by a natural bottom line shit detector.

Yet despite the almost constant reevaluation that Don has done, there are important constants—particularly his belief that we must reconsider the way we use time in the classroom and create spaces big enough for children to become obsessed with what they learn. At one point he says:

> It's so important to know what it means to know something well. And until you know at least one thing well, you don't respect the demands of other disciplines are. Things just get so watered down. Kids hate learning because they've never gotten far enough to love something—because they know something about it.

We can also see in the interview the high expectations Graves has for students. Too often writing process work is pictured as supportive, nurturing, tolerant—and fundamentally *soft*. If students have almost unlimited choice, if the teacher is merely a shadowy facilitator, where is the rigor in the approach? The teacher Graves describes in this interview is one who actively challenges (or sometimes "crowds") students. "Unlimited choice," he says, "is no choice at all."

The essays in this collection illustrate enduring themes in the writing process movement and new directions for teaching and teacher research. In her classic study, *The Composing Processes of 12th Graders*, Janet Emig (1971) made an almost clairvoyant observation about teacher education. A decade before the Bay Area Writing Project began, she argued that writing teachers should write—learning from inside the processes they and their students go through. The *Workshop* series was created as a forum for teacher writing but, thus far, only for essays on teaching and learning—schooltalk. As anyone who has attended a writing project knows, some of the most exciting breakthroughs occur when teachers take on other genres—fiction, poetry, the personal essay. I wanted to make space for that writing as well. In the section, "Teachers as Writers," I included poems by Teresa Butchko and Sherry Falco, and a personal essay by Ann-Marie Oomen, each accompanied by a commentary describing the process of composition.

I also looked for essays that describe the *emotional underlife* of the writing process. In *Workshop 4*, I criticize the emotionally sanitized versions of writing process/whole language teaching. We are often trapped in success stories, carefully cropped pictures that ignored failure and sometimes even difficulty. The essays by Vicki Swartz and Kathleen Mahan are candid and moving meditations that do not ignore the difficulties of their work. Another kind of story that is often missing is that of African-American teachers. As Lisa Delpit (1988) pointedly reminds us in her influential essay, the writing process movement has been led, almost exclusively, by white, middle-class educators. In response to Delpit's challenge, JoAnn Curtis reports on a conversation with Dawn Harris-Martine and Isoke Nia, two African-American teachers and teacher-educators in New York City.

In *New Questions/New Directions*, three essays represent new thinking about the teaching of writing. Sherry Seale Swain's study of portfolios in a primary classroom is an exemplary piece of teacher research that carefully examines the criteria young children use to discuss their writing. Barbara Bagge-Rynerson's piece shows how a reflective teacher confronts a problem. She found that her first- and second-grade students were giving only perfunctory answers in their reading journals (a more common problem than the professional literature would lead us to believe). She interviewed her students about the problem and discovered that while *she* saw the journal as a place to explore reactions, *they* saw it as checking up on them. As a result of her survey, she shifted away from using interrogating questions in her own responses. Maureen Barbieri's essay, "Kristin's Story: A Moral Voice Emerges" makes a useful connection between fiction-writing and the developmental work of Carol Gilligan and her associates (some of it conducted at Laurel School where Maureen taught). According to Gilligan the moral development of adolescent girls is often limited by an overpowering desire to fit into social groups. Girls at this age may lose the boldness they had in fifth and sixth grades. Barbieri shows how fiction writing can provide a vicarious space for adolescent girls to experiment with more independent decision-making.

Another new direction is the way teachers are increasingly integrating writing and the arts. Maybe it is an inevitable law of evolution that we begin by compartmentalizing. At any rate, in early writing process classrooms, writing was pretty well segregated from the rest of the curriculum. Although it was clear that young children drew before they wrote, drawing (and talking) was considered *rehearsal* for writing. This view unintentionally diminished the role of oral language and the arts, turning them into preliminaries for writing. The teachers in *Writing and the Arts* take a much more interactive view, closer to "*symbol-weaving*," where various symbol systems (drawing, music, gesture, movement, oral language, written language) play off each other. Mona Halaby connects writing with drama, Lisa Lenz with oral expression, Susan Blecher and Kathy Jaffee with music and performance, and Katherine Link and Karen Ernst with art. The final essay in this section, "Writing Class as Medicine Wheel" by Peggy Voss is a moving description of a classroom that reminds us of the primordial importance of oral storytelling.

To read essays like Voss' is to marvel, once again, at the creativity of teachers and to recognize the ways in which educators like Graves have fostered change by their profound respect for classroom practitioners. But I wonder about the next step. Where do we go from here? It may well be that we are in the second phase of the writing process movement. The first was instructional—developing classroom approaches that foster literacy learning. The second and hardest phase may be political—combatting the institutional forces that prevent effective literacy learning. Although we will always need to refine our understanding of writing, it is fair to say, that we know—right now—how to do the job. We know children need to write regularly in a variety of genre; we know they need supportive and useful critical responses; we know they need to reflect on what they are doing; we know wide and careful reading is essential for good writing; and we know that for writing to be meaningful, students need to write about their lives and what matters to them. I don't mean to argue that doing this, in every classroom, for every student, is easy. It's hard work. But there is no great secret to be unlocked about how we should do our work.

Working against this type of instruction is a different set of assumptions drawn, usually unintentionally, from the factory model of learning (the governor of my state refers to graduating seniors as "outputs" of the educational system). Those operating within this metaphor typically overrate standardization (often confusing it with standards) and are uncomfortable with the diversity that comes of teacher initiative. When forming curricula, administrators ask the fatally misdirected question, "What should our students know?" The answer is usually some form of "everything," and teachers are saddled with fragmented *coverage* curricula.

To resist this factory approach, teachers must break out of the isolation that is a part of institutional life—visit each others' classrooms, form study groups, read professional articles, develop presentations, and share classroom stories.

And, perhaps most painfully for us all, we have to accept the fact that institutional change does not come about without some form of conflict.

But there is a violence that comes of being silent, of acquiescing. There is violence to us and to our students when unwise, top-down curricular decisions prevent us from practicing our craft. There is a violence that occurs when we don't get beyond the grumbling and the private complaining. And there is a moral energy that comes of honest conflict, when we fight for the space we need to do our job.

This marks the end of my editorship of the *Workshop* series. I hope to get on with more of my own writing in the near future. I want to thank the many teachers who have submitted their work to this series. The series will be in the skillful hands of Maureen Barbieri and Linda Rief, both contributors to the *Workshop* series. I wish them well.

T.N.

References

Delpit, Lisa. 1988. "The Silenced Dialogue: Power and Pedagogy in Educating Other People's Children." *Harvard Educational Review*, 58: 280–298.

Emig, Janet. 1971. *The Composing Processes of Twelfth Graders*. Urbana, Illinois: National Council of Teachers of English.

The View from the Mountains
A MORNING WITH DONALD GRAVES

THOMAS NEWKIRK
University of New Hampshire
Durham, New Hampshire

*T*en years have passed since the publication of Donald Graves' *Writing: Teachers and Children at Work*, a huge best seller that has helped revolutionize writing instruction in this country (though that revolution is far from over). Even before this book came out, Don often said, "You always have to ask, what will happen if what you want to have happen, happens?" This was more than a tongue-twister. One of the things that can happen is that a writer becomes trapped in earlier publications, identified with positions he no longer holds.

So, I thought it was time to spend a morning with Don to explore the roots of his ideas about teaching and the changes those ideas have gone through. We talked on a beautiful August day in his home in Jackson, New Hampshire, where he has moved since his retirement. The north side of the house is a bank of windows, providing a hypnotic view of the White Mountains with Mount Washington off to the far left. I thought that in this house I'd never get any work done. I'd just look out the windows.

After breakfast, we talked.

Personal Histories

TN: I'd like to start out with the idea that our philosophies are disguised autobiographies. I was wondering if in some ways your approach to writing was autobiographical, a retelling of your own learning story?

DG: Yes, it is. We all have had both good and poor experiences and it's so easy to teach in such a way that we try to reenact the good ones and negate the bad ones. The only problem is that there's often some wisdom in the bad ones, and you spend your life escaping those, not really dealing with them.

I had a terrible experience when I was a senior in college. I was struggling with becoming a conscientious objector. My best friend, Ted Davey, saw a little white slip in his box. We kidded him. We thought, "Gee, he's dating girls now." (He was scared to death of girls.)

"Hey, who is she, Ted?" And he opens the box and reads, "You are hereby ordered to report to active duty."

He said, "They can't do that." Eight weeks later he was dead. Shot by a sniper in Korea before he saw action. So I built that into my struggle with conscientious objection. I was very much into Tolstoy, and, in a paper, I paralleled Teddy and Bolkonsky in *War and Peace*, waiting to go into battle. He never got there, either; he was hit while his unit was ready to go into a cavalry charge. There's a steady struggle with "Should I kill?" that's really enacted in Pierre.

So I'm going through this whole struggle, and I get that paper back—"D+. Please change your typewriter ribbon." And I just went berserk. I've looked at the paper since then—it *was* bad. On the other hand, it was an honest struggle, and there are some good parts to it. But the fact that there was absolutely no response to the content really got me.

I didn't become a conscientious objector. I did go into the Coast Guard, which was a fairly good guarantee that I wouldn't kill anyone. But I struggled for a long time after that, sort of on the front burner, trying to learn everything. Trying to prove that I *was* a learner. I've always loved to learn, and I spent four years just learning all kinds of things—anatomy, physiology, Russian, psychology—on my own.

When I ultimately ended up in teaching, which I did not want to do when I left Bates, I above all wanted to have environments where students could explore what they wanted to know, to really take off, use time differently. And I did. And it worked.

The flip side of that, however, is there were particular things that kids needed to have more discipline on, to learn. The professor who gave me the D+ was right about some things. And it's only been in the last three years that I've seen that. I also had a professor who was almost a complete fascist in his approach to teaching. He had a Master's degree and some gutty soul (who had all A's) asked him at the end of the semester why he didn't have his doctorate. He said, "Who would examine me?" And for some weird reason, under that guy I thrived. So I encountered these mystifying people who were absolutely obnoxious fascists—from whom I learned a lot.

I couldn't teach that way, ever. On the other hand, people sometimes need this sternness. So, there is a yin and yang to your history, which is certainly reenacted in my own life. There are things we need to expect of kids. And there are times when we need to say, "Do it now." For some kids, the choices must be quite explicit. This stuff about absolute choice—that's no choice. That's the weakness of it.

TN: What caused this reconsideration?

DG: I realized that I was going in and saying to someone, "This isn't right." I'd be in the classroom and say, "There are some questions you ought to ask." I wasn't subtle about it. And then I realized that I was starting to compensate through my own practice, but I was never putting it in writing. I was realizing that I was practicing differently—especially with doctoral students. If something was bad, you just couldn't say, "It's your choice." It's time to speak about it as it is. So in my own practice, I realized that I was filling in where filling in was needed.

Portfolios

TN: One of the things I noticed in *Build a Literate Classroom* was the importance of the word "history." It is really a key word in that book. Histories of pieces of writing, of learners. I didn't see that emphasis in some of the earlier books. Could you say something about the importance of histories?

DG: It's funny. If you look at your history, at the things you know how to do well, you learned to do them through "learning binges." You really laid into them, became obsessed by them. You read all of the books of some author; you worked night and day on it. It required that to get into the subject. In theatre, in coaching, it's when a teacher has very intense, extended relationships with people that something significant happens.

And what we do for learning in schools is that we bleed it to death. State curricula say so many minutes for X. But nobody learns that way. It's quite antithetical. So both autobiographically, but also in talking to people, I find that they learn in very different ways.

TN: It seems to me there is also a sense of history embedded in the notion of "portfolio."

DG: Yes. There can be. It's like I have a history but do I know how to read it? So you have a repository of stuff, but it can be just that. And that's my fear about portfolios. They're only going to be good if people know how to read them. And to some degree I'll distort it in the reading, but that's the challenge of teaching, to have different ways in which you can learn to read your history and the work in it—and to know how to read it as a writer would read it. Or get different perspectives from different people on how it would be read. I don't think that job is being done.

TN: How do you teach that? If you're asking students to collect things they've done, things they have written, things they've read, how do you teach someone to read that history?

DG: Number one, I'm constantly demonstrating myself. I'm trying to demonstrate above all the kinds of questions I ask, the curiosities I have, the resolutions I make: "Well, I have to work on this." But I think it's also in mini-lessons. I think there are various elements: "Let's just take a minute and look at how authors begin things. Get the trade book you're reading right now. You're writing fiction, OK, get the writer of fiction you're reading now." (I like people to be reading in the same genre they're writing a little more than is now being done.) "You have a character that first appears here. Take a look at it. How do your characters appear?"

I think we need to be that directive in calling attention to all different kinds of things that authors do. And the sad thing about fiction is it's so *laissez faire* in schools. There's very little teaching done in fiction; it's like anything goes, which is absolute nonsense. For me, it's the most demanding medium to write in. I mean, you're God. You're creating people. If you want to create a person, you've got a responsibility there. You can't insist on more than you can get, but you need to begin raising questions about characters.

> A kid writes, "He pulled out a gun and shot him." I ask, "What did he do that for?" And the kid says, "He was bad."
> "Can you tell me more about that?"
> "Well, he was ugly."

"You mean they kill people because they are ugly?"

"Geez, Mr. Graves, this is fiction. You don't need to answer questions like that."

There are real responsibilities there. To me, that's the real redefinition of "ownership," which was a decent term in its time, but it needs redefinition. That is, I have responsibilities with this house. I can't just do anything I want to it. When I write, I have a responsibility to tell the truth—and that takes work. So I'm probing for what truth he's working at here. And I think we have to crowd kids on these fronts—and that's what I mean about being more directive, more confrontational. And actually I think kids like that.

TN: And it also seems to me that those questions that ask students to consider their writing create a sense in the student as somebody with a past, a present, and a future.

DG: Absolutely. And until you can help a kid have a past, who cares about plans? It's all present. And I think that's been the problem with kids as we've worked with them. The kid says, "I think I'll write about a Teenage Mutant Ninja Turtle today." And it's like the kid exists only in the present. The folders at least contributed to some sense of beginning histories. But we didn't use the folders; it was a collection. And the kid who struggles most in school is a kid who is a prisoner of the present.

TN: Do you think that's a reflection of the culture? We live in a culture that tends to be dominated by the moment.

DG: Absolutely. The good thing that writing has done since we've been working on it is that more kids are having a sense of past, but it's been amorphous. We haven't taken advantage of it.

TN: So that by looking at what you have done in the past you get a direction for future writing. You have a sense of continuity of yourself as a learner.

DG: Right. And it happens with a piece. A kid's working on a piece and he's stuck. I say, "How did you happen to get into this?" So I immediately start to reenact the past. "Oh, I forgot, I was a goalie and we won in overtime and it was the last second and this kid came in on me and I stopped him." And he had gotten on to something else. So much of teaching is re-orienting the writer to the origin, the wellspring of the piece.

TN: So the folder instead of becoming an archive . . .

DG: It becomes a useful history. It's a way of reading the archive, of saying, 'This is where I have been. This is where I want to go.' And without the 'this is where I want to go', the kid is still in the present tense.

School Reform

TN: I want to go back to the "learning binge." It was Eliot Eisner who said that he hated well-rounded people because they could roll in any direction. There are certain passions that need to be indulged. You said that your own rhythm of learning was that you become obsessed, absorbed with a subject. What structural changes in schools are necessary for that to happen?

DG: The best example I saw was in Scotland, where starting about age nine, kids could elect, or be elected to, independent study. And there would be this block of time when kids could read independently under the guidance of a tutor, quite common in the English system. Only everyone in the entire system, including the superintendent or Chief School Officer, had these various specialties. So that if you elected X, you knew exactly who would take you on. And that was administration, teachers, specials—everyone had all these areas; there were some kids, the chief school officers told me, who had ⅓ to ½ of their schooling in this independent study. And these were the kids who really busted the A and O level national exams.

I think that we need to seriously look at the meaning of independent studies and start to build them in earlier. Let them get into these areas. I did some of this when I was a principal, when I was working with specialties. Everyone in the school had a specialty: faculty, cafeteria workers, custodians. Everyone was pursuing some area of study, simultaneous to the curriculum, and time was given to that.

It's so important to know what it means to know something well. And until you know at least one thing well, you don't respect the demands of other disciplines. Things just get so watered down. Kids hate learning because they've never gotten far enough to love something—because they know something about it.

TN: It seems like almost anybody who has done anything well, whether it be business, whether it would be writing, would say something similar to what you've said. You need passion, you need to get lost in a project. I would think there would be agreement over that. What's keeping schools from allowing that to happen?

DG: Oh. First of all, in order for people to use time independently, you have to decentralize an operation. And schools are more centralized today than ever before. And they're centralized in several ways. The two people who control curriculum more than any other people in a school system are the business officer (or, in some cases, the assistant superintendent for management and business) and the person in charge of testing. Those two people do more to control a school system than any two other people. You can have curriculum meetings forever, and one decision by one guy on the budget or one guy on when busses will run can outflank you in the twinkling of an eye. There are some attempts to have budget control strictly by the building, but they last for about 18 months and they're gone. There's just so much centralization.

And a second limiting force is school law. School attorneys are so anxious about how easily people can be sued because X supervision wasn't in place. Nancie Atwell's kids (at the Center for Teaching and Learning) leave the school for mile hikes; a mile hike on history, a mile hike on flora and fauna, a mile hike for physical fitness. This would drive people nuts in a school system because of all the liability problems.

These two areas just have to be rethought; it's not an excuse for not doing it. But there's a central tendency that's pulling back innovation into a very conservative nonthinking, non-risk-taking mode. If you live in the contexts of no-risk finance, no risk of liability, and no risk of coming out with low scores, how can you have an environment for learning that requires high risk?

TN: OK. But a conservative would say, "*I agree with you, Don. And the only way we can do this is to have separate schools that are not public schools that can challenge the model of the public schools. It's just not going to work within the existing school bureaucracies because everyone has a stake in the system. You have to create these other structures that challenge the public schools and develop newer models because they are less restricted. They'll be smaller; they won't have all the mandates and baggage that the public schools have.*" That's the conservative argument.

DG: The irony is that in the Bush proposal we're going to have in each congressional district the opportunity to create a new school, a new concept of a school. It was a good idea. The trouble is, when Secretary of Education Alexander was at

UNH, I said to him, "That's a wonderful idea. Why is it that you can't also have alternative approaches to assessment in order to allow a school not only to try new ways of learning, but new ways of thinking about learning and how we look to see if different kinds of learning are taking place." And he sort of said, "Oh, that's interesting."

Research in Children's Writing

TN: I want to take you back to the study in Atkinson (which led to *Writing: Teachers and Children at Work*). Looking back at your NIE study of children's writing, 1978–1980, what were the most important things that you found out?

DG: I think the most important thing for me was to get close to kids and their thinking. We just can't do enough of that kind of work. Kids can make decisions; they can make clear decisions. Kids have an energy for learning that we underestimate all the time. Above all, if you merely give data back to teachers about what went on in their classrooms, they know what to do with it. It's just that most of us don't have the opportunity to be continually informed by the ways our kids think. That's a very powerful cycle: to teach and then to have someone say, "This is what I saw today." But often when someone is in a class supervising someone, the focus is more on the teacher than on the kids. And if you put the lens on the kids, that is a far more powerful educator of the teacher than focusing on the teacher.

There are also things I've come to question. I was convinced then that there were sequences of development, and I was trying to nail them down more than they could be nailed down. I think that was one of the greatest weaknesses of the study, and in my subsequent writing there is this strong suggestion that learning is always these little tiny increments of things—and I was wrong. When I look in Linda Rief's classroom, in Nancie Atwell's classroom, where there is this incredible engagement, where there are high challenges to kids—to the entire classroom and to individual kids—I've seen kids make these huge leaps that are inexplicable in terms of developmental sequences. But then that's when I shifted to conditions for learning rather than methods for teaching and stages of development. I think that's a major shift for me.

TN: Say something more about that shift.

DG: That's sort of a big span in there. It took a long time for this shift to happen. I was heavily influenced by Piaget for a lot longer than I realized—and there's still some of that there. You don't suddenly do X before B. But take Mary Ann Wessell's class. A kid picks up and reads Lloyd Alexander, and all of a sudden he starts writing like Lloyd Alexander. Explain that developmentally! He just suddenly puts all these things together. It would take a hundred mini-lessons to teach a kid to do that. You see, that's where the developmental model falls apart. I was so method-centered back then. People liked my work because first I said do this, then that, then that. I tried to steer away from it, but there is a certain amount of prescription in *Writing: Teachers and Children at Work*. I guess when you're trying something for the first time you may need a one-two-three to just get your toe in the door. But it's so seductive in terms of publication. You give all these one-two-threes—and you're trapped in your own publishing.

TN: In *Build a Literate Classroom*, you talk about the writing conference and how you might have oversold it. Is that a part of what you're saying?

DG: I don't think it's part of the developmental issue, but that is definitely a shift. The problem with the conference was I tried to do everything through it. And teachers were coming to me saying, "Oh my gosh, I'm just sprinting around the room." And I knew something was wrong. But I couldn't put my finger on it. And this is where Lucy Calkins coming in with the mini-lesson concept was a real help. I think that was a major contribution. That took the stress off the conference. And then I began to see more clearly how a few conferences teach quite a few people. And then there were all kinds of other ways that you teach: when kids share, you teach. The other side was that as kids get more proficient, they share with each other. But still there was too much in the conference and there was too much that the teacher had to do there. And that's definitely a flaw. In the new book I'm writing now (a revision of *Writing: Teachers and Children at Work*), I'm striking the section on conferences—I may have gone too far.

TN: Striking it?

DG: Yeah. There will be examples of conferences. The transaction that goes on in the conference is right. I feel strongly about that. And the whole intent of the conference is to put the kid on his own, allow the kid to speak, listen to the kid, and learn—having the kid teach you. That's good. But the kid didn't need the teacher as much as I thought. And conditions teach, more than I realized. So take the strain off the conference.

TN: In the early work the conference was *the* major instructional event of the class.

DG: The problem was the design of the study would lead you to end up there. We were studying children and their development. So along comes the teacher, and we are getting this rich stuff through the conferences, through talking to kids. Plus we had the overlay of Don Murray. We were very heavily influenced by Murray—the conference approach and his notion of what writers do. So we superimposed a university model onto the classroom. And because we saw good data there, and we saw very good learning by the kids—we weren't attending to the *social interactions* among children. And if you don't get the data, they don't exist. Which is always the great trap of research.

TN: But in terms of what you saw—even given the limitations of the lens—what surprised you? What's lasted with you?

DG: Well, certainly the importance of talk. Kids should be explaining what they're doing far more than they have a chance to do. And that is instructive to the kids. (Pause.)

I know one of the things that came out of our early work that was a partial mistake—partial, I'll say—was revision. We were amazed that kids did change things because Carl Bereiter said they didn't do it before the fifth grade. We had data showing that young children were making revisions. But just because they were revising, was more revision better? Probably not.

On the other hand, it was important that kids wanted to fool around with stuff, and they did a lot of fooling around with stuff when we weren't there that was good. And, I think, too, that although I had it in my original dissertation, choice is still a pretty important thing—and I think we established that.

Another thing that snuck in, although other people were working on it—Carol Chomsky, Ed Henderson, the Beers—was invented spelling. I think that's an important thing. On the other hand, I think it lasts too long.

TN: Do you think teachers thought that maybe it would correct itself and they didn't need to do anything?

DG: That's true. And I think there are still words in the English language that are bugaboos you need to learn. Pat McLure does it. There are words that are important for everybody to learn, and then there are your words. You need to learn both. And politically in our culture you're dead if you can't spell.

The Dangers of Orthodoxy

TN: Several years ago you gave a talk, later published, claiming that the "enemy was orthodoxy." Is that still true?

DG: Yes. We aren't self-critical enough. We just aren't.

TN: You sound pretty self-critical today.

DG: Yeah. I've changed. For example, in the last two sequences in the doctoral seminar [at UNH] I really pushed people to come in with the opposite side of the debate. But we're still a little too self-congratulatory.

The thing that bothers me so much about the whole language movement is that it is not self-critical. I have dire predictions for the movement. There's been terrific stuff done, and there's been a belief in teachers that has been strong. But there has to be more self-criticism, publicly, far greater intellectual demand on the movement than we've had. And I think to some degree that could be a criticism of the early work we did with children's writing. Maybe that's part of our maturity, becoming more self-critical. I hope so.

TN: What kinds of self-criticism might go on in the whole language movement?

DG: It's the same thing that I was trying to nail when I did my piece on 'Let's get rid of the orthodoxies.' At every point, we need to stop and say, "OK, what are our orthodoxies right now?" One of the orthodoxies you slip into is Big Book Orthodoxies. There is a place somewhere, sometime, for big books.

There's the Good Unit Orthodoxy. There is a place, somewhere, sometime, for good units, these umbrella-type projects. But to build a whole curriculum strictly around those is another orthodoxy.

I also see within the movement this Have-You-Read-This-Book-Yet one-upmanship in children's literature that is just plain silly. There are so many people walking around feeling guilty because they have not read so and so. There is a fierce competition.

So I hear people coming up with these little statements,

these little code words, to see if other people are whole language people. Like these little Baptist tracts, "Are You Saved?" kind of mentality. Definitely, there were those elements in the writing work early on. Certain people in the movement gave those little codes out. Probably I did myself. But I also see it when I see people get up and condemn, *carte blanche*, all the people who do X. I just don't think that helps anyone. They are signs of old age in a movement and they have to be called by name.

TN: And like the skills teaching that is always condemned—that you teach everything in context. It seems to me that mini-lessons and more direct instruction, some of the things you have mentioned—that even that orthodoxy would have to be tempered in some way. Do kids always get things in context?

DG: Let's say a kid has written something, and you say, "Find a piece where you have dialogue. We're going to work on dialogue and quotations. OK." It is within the context of that piece, but temporally it is out of context. It's sort of half a step toward context, which I think is important. On the other hand I have to realize that probably I'm not scratching the kid where he itches today. But we're going to do it anyway.

The Revision of *Writing: Teachers and Children at Work*

TN: I want to get into the revisions of *Writing: Teachers and Children at Work*. Here you have the book that has sold about 180,000 copies. It's easily the most widely bought, widely influential book on children's writing ever written. Now you've agreed to do a revision. How do you go about it?

DG: It's funny. At first I just didn't want to do it. Philippa [Stratton, of Heinemann Educational Books] came up to the house the first week of August. I said, "Philippa, I appreciate you coming up here, but it's just that in retirement I want to go ahead, I don't want to go back." But I agreed to sit down and by the first of September (1992) I promised to make a decision. And so I sat down, and I went through it quickly. I started looking at the chapters. And I said, "This job is enormous. This goes. That goes. That goes."

TN: Did you reread the book?

DG: I started to, and it was too painful. It's so funny. You see, the book is being used differently now. It's being used more for preservice teachers, people who need to get a toehold and just get started. I looked at the book and said, "My lord, there

are so many things that are fundamental that are not stressed."
So I started to look at what the fundamentals are. And I start
right away with "Let's take a look at our roots. I'll do it with
you." That's the principle I have in the book; whatever I ask
you to do, I'll do. And so I look at my roots.

So to come to your question, I just went through and said,
"These are all the things you need to have as basic building
blocks to get in. Just don't miss these."

TN: These building blocks weren't there in the first book?

DG: They were sort of there, but just not as naked. For instance,
there's learning from children in the book, but I'll be more
specific in the revision. There are what I call "actions." For
example:

> "Ask the child to bring something to school that she knows about.
> Help the child to teach you about it. Where possible, tape record
> your sessions."

> "Observe five children on the playground or in a music, physical
> education, or art class. Look for something each knows how to
> do, and then ask them how they learned to do it."

So there is a lot more learning from children around the
writing—as opposed to just directly going to the writing.
There are different ways of learning from kids, particularly
learning what they *can do*. The hardest kid to teach is the kid
who sees in your face that he has no potential. So how can
you come to it with a sense of rich potential?

Then I stop cold and give a conceptual chapter. "What is
this thing called 'writing', anyway." What researchers say
about writing, what expert teachers say about writing, what
writers say about writing . . . And what is this thing called
'writing' in the field of communication? So we look at writing
from a range of circles.

And the next part is "Learn from children about writing."
There is a lot of time spent on learning. See, you're not teach-
ing yet. Just spend time learning and the teaching will come.
But just get into these learning experiences. In the first edition,
I was trying to get people off the mark, quickly into the teaching.
Now there are teaching opportunities in here, but you don't
suddenly have to have a whole class doing things all at once.
We'll get to the doing soon enough. So the first part is just a lot
of picking up information, learning, getting it down.

TN: You know, there's a story my uncle told. He was a gambler
in the service and he would send home money to my dad to

deposit in the bank from the navy. He didn't gamble for a year. He watched everybody else gamble. He saw what people did, how they bluffed, how they tipped their hand. So when he started he made five or six thousand dollars a year. That's a good metaphor, I think.

DG: My brother did the same thing. My brother used to go up to the barn where the men gambled on Saturday afternoon, playing poker. And George, from the age of 12 up until 16, had four years of watching those guys. And each year he bugged my mom, "Let me play, let me play." And my mother, finally at 16, said, "Let him play, they'll teach him a lesson." (Laughs.) It was the old men—my Uncle Nelson, and bankers from the town, heads of businesses—and the kid, my brother who wanted to go to college. It didn't work. My brother usually won. Finally, the president of the bank, Pat Carpenter, said, "George, I don't know what it is that you've got, but it's something the bank needs." At the end of the year he was head teller. The next year he was into mortgages, and within six years he was vice president.

TN: There's a moral in there somewhere.

DG: Observation: it's not a luxury. And as long as it's structured so that you really are in position to learn things, observation really is useful.

Poetry

TN: I want to shift a little bit to my own sense of your change as a writer. How has your experience of writing poetry changed your sense of what teaching writing is about?

DG: I think it's from the poetry that the notion of being in a constant state of composition has dawned on me. You see poems all the time, particularly when I ran into John Jerome, author of *Stonework*. He doesn't write poetry, but he has that awareness all the time. He's constantly seeing something and saying, "How come?" "What's that for?" It really starts to make you raise questions of a more fundamental nature. It's seeing things in intense nuggets and then being able to fool around with them in a short space that gives you an intensity that's important to me. I do it now in my journal. I have intensity in the journal each day. Or in my "literate occasions" that I introduce in *Discover Your Own Literacy*. That's been real important. I think it's led to richer living. It's helped me to understand more what writing can do.

Working with poetry has also made me more aware of the line. There's something about the line. When Annie Dillard was here, someone yelled out a question to her: "What does it take to be a writer?" She answered, "Do you like sentences?" I'm realizing that it comes down to that, and it started with poetry. The line is very important in a poem, and the line has become more important to me. I've always liked one-liners but I didn't really live it.

TN: Isn't it strange that at the age of 62 (I don't mean to be offensive), you're finally getting into this? What was it that kept you from writing poetry?

DG: I don't know. I think the rush of things was too much. Maybe old age. You start to get a feel for what's important. It's better to slow down and live life more intensely than it is to be so frenetic and lose out on things, and I've certainly realized that since May and retirement. I'm getting much more done now because I am slowing down and starting to ask more critical questions—maybe because I have time to. I've written, since May, the equivalent of three books, just in my journal. I write about 2,000 words a day. Very rapid writing but it's sort of loose writing. Then in the midst I'll say, "Boom, this is it." So there's a lot of covering, but a lot of intensity. A lot of writing while I'm reading books. I sit down and have the book here, and I go, "That reminds me of this," and I write.

TN: Has this changed the way you think writing should be taught in schools?

DG: Slow down. It does pop up in *Build a Literate Classroom*. Stand in the room and look at kids and ask, "Who are the kids that will read on their own and will write on their own?", just based on what they're doing now. I think we have to ask questions like that. And to start slowing down, and having environments that really allow kids to explore, make mistakes, and talk. So that in the long run they'll be lifetime readers and writers. So few are. We've just absolutely failed in that regard. And I think it's possible. There are good teachers who have demonstrated that it is possible. And let's focus on those good teachers.

Good teachers have kids who are continuing to think when they're not in class; the kid's burned up with the subject when he's at home, on the bus, walking. Now that's the real use of time. Good teachers have exploded the time/space concepts of the room. Time on task? Can't tell in a good room. You can only tell beyond and in the course of a lifetime. And I think we know enough now to say what lasts. You want them to read at home, let them read in school. Very simple, but it works. And that's good use of time.

Teacher Research

TN: One last question. What question would you like to see teachers asking, as part of teacher research? What question or advice would you give to teachers who are beginning to do research?

DG: I can't say what the questions are, but I think it's important for teacher to keep a notebook or journal for jottings, for a time, to help look for a question. Just star questions of "How come?" "How come this kid did this?" "How come schools are this way?" "What worked for me yesterday? I wonder why it worked?" Look at some kids to find out the things they know, and then start asking them how they knew that. Set yourself up for starting to learn and to just take moments to jot notes, go through a good process of learning about your scene and reflecting on it. After a certain period, be willing to sit down and talk to someone who is going through a similar process. Talk about the things that interest you based on certain evidences that you've seen. It's not one single evidence. It's just something that's started to emerge that's interested you. And you start learning a little more about it.

Don't try to be formal too soon. Above all, enter into it with another person or persons. And continue to talk. Then after six months or nine months, a couple of questions will emerge that you want to go on. I find that people try to rush into it too soon, do it alone, without bouncing ideas off others. Just agree that it's going to take time. Get into some readings of other people who are thinking in those same areas. And then afterward, talk with people who are knowledgeable. Enter into it as a two-or-three-year venture. What's the rush?

TN: It's the same advice you give to the kids. Slow down.

DG: Slow down. Slow down. Enjoy the trip. If you're willing to commit yourself to longer periods of time, you're going to have fun on the way. And it ought to be fun. Disciplined fun.

THE TEACHER
AS WRITER

WRITING "SANCTUARY"

THERESA BUTCHKO
Lake Ridge Academy
North Ridgeville, Ohio

I missed my boys. Nothing helped. Neither the warmth of my colleagues nor the high I felt from being in the University of New Hampshire Writing Program could alleviate my longing to hold my two little boys. I explained to my class on Friday afternoon how, when I was stressed, I would look in the boys' room and watch them sleep, and at times even sneak in behind Thommy, my four year old, and snuggle close until my breathing and pulse slowed to his naturally calm pace.

The next Monday morning when I told Tom Newkirk, "You'll never guess what I did this weekend," he responded immediately, "You wrote a poem—about your son." I was stunned. The class knew I had had a phobia about writing poetry since I was eight years old and was rejected for publication by *Highlights Magazine*. I asked, "How did you know?" Tom said simply, "Because what you described Friday felt like a poem."

I guess that was the key to my ignition. I had an experience I wanted to share, explain, and, more importantly, to reexperience for myself. When I sat at the word processor I began to brainstorm. I naturally think in similes and metaphors. I study the faces of strangers until I can figure out which film star they vaguely remind me of. So, when I began to think how I felt and looked when I was the most stressed, my body began to hunch over, my brow squinched, and my mind flashed to Charles Laughton in his burlap cloak frantically tolling the church bell. It clicked. I was Quasi Modo. Then, when I began to think about the contrasting serenity I felt in my sons' room, I thought quite naturally that it felt like a church, like a *sanctuary*.

I tingled. There was a link. A connection. I had now transformed my metaphor into an extended metaphor.

Unfortunately for me, however, I had unleashed within myself the metaphor from Hell. It took over every aspect of the poem. I described my stress in redundant and forced detail:

> I hover over the blur before me
> Straining to relieve myself of one more
> Deadline
> demand
> heaped
> onto my back
> But I cannot.
>
> It is a part of me now
> And it draws me out of sync with myself
> Transforming me into a mutant.

At that point I was no longer interested in relaying an experience; I was concentrating on how many times I could work in the Modo motif. I am embarrassed to remember that while writing the "Deadline" stanza, I actually thought to myself, "Neat. I made a hump."

I was so proud of my original draft and its clever use of this sophisticated literary device. I couldn't wait to read it to Tom. I remember looking up as I read the last line of my first draft and searching my mentor's face for approval. But Tom smiled and then looked more querulous than impressed. "Geez, Teresa," he finally said, "I don't even know your kid and you want me to believe he's Jesus Christ!"

I had to laugh. I knew right away what he meant. The poem wasn't real. I went off to the word processor to regain control of my poem.

I studied every line of the poem and asked myself, "Is this how I really felt at the time, or was this phrase or word put in for effect?" One egregiously bad verse was the first to go:

> SANCTUARY! I shout within
>
> Hobbling down the dark hall
> Strange bells tolling in my ears
> I find my church and the object of my worship

First, I never shouted "Sanctuary" within or without. I never hobbled down a dark hall. I love my sons, but they are not objects of my worship. The entire verse became one line:

Ears ringing, I hobble to his room to find my sanctuary.

Other parts of the metaphor were more difficult to let go. I envisioned walking into the room and seeing the shadows against the wall. I originally wrote,

> The commissioned moon, half covered by clouds, covers his walls with a mosaic of shadow and light.

I later changed "covers" to "paints" both to avoid repetition in the line and to enhance the idea of the room being a sanctuary. But, I later conceded that God did not commission the moon any more than he commissioned Michelangelo to decorate Thommy's room. It wasn't real, so it distanced the reader who at best would have said, "Um, clever." That was a real turning point for me, realizing that "clever" was not the mood I was after. "Clever" is not a mood at all. When I decided that my main focus was to convey the serenity I feel from the simplicity of my children sleeping, editing became less painful. I wanted the reader to feel the calm, not notice the poet.

I spent over twenty hours working on the poem, carefully eyeing redundancy. Why not "spastic lashes" rather than "spastically fluttering lashes?" What else would spastic lashes do but flutter? Did I need to explain that demands "drew me out of sync with myself," or was that obvious with the rest of the poem? I had anyone who would read the poem tell me what they saw. One friend asked, "How can a 'jutting neck recoil'?" I couldn't see it myself, so I changed the line to

> My jutting neck realigns to fit
> his downy head under my chin.

I worked to make the images clear, simple, and honest.

Ironically, one line I rushed to omit was

> The wafer of air between his lips.

I remember when I originally wrote that line I thought I might have been going too far with the extended metaphor. Who will ever get the tie to communion wafers? But just as I went to push "delete," I looked at the line again. My mind flashed to Thommy's face, his lips barely open, and I could feel the little wisp of air coming from his mouth. The line made me see and feel, so I kept it. Even though as originally intended, it was a bad idea. I think I stumbled onto a nice line because it was small, simple, and consistent with the tone of the poem.

Eight drafts later I turned in my final revision to Tom with a full-page letter asking specifically about what I should keep and what else I should delete. He wrote back, "Put it in the drawer now. I don't think more revising at this point is appropriate." That was perhaps the most difficult part of writing this poem— putting it away. I will never be completely satisfied with any piece I write. The process was so intoxicating I got to relive even more intensely a special memory.

The boys are older now. I still stand in the doorway and watch them sleep. At times I pull the poem out of its drawer and replay it in my mind and come in sync with its *slow waltz time.*

Sanctuary

Hunched under the fluorescent glare
I slump
Present day Quasi Modo
A freak of nature born of stress and fatigue.
Lips stretched white over clenched teeth,
Deep ridged brow over spastic lashes,
Ears ringing, I hobble to his room to find my sanctuary.

The moon, half hidden by clouds, covers his walls with shadow
    and light.
There on his sheets he lies, arms stretched outward, opened to
    the breeze.
I lie beside him.
He unconsciously folds toward me,
    his small hand just touching my arm.
I study his face
        the creamy smoothness of his lids and brow
        the stillness of his lashes
        the wafer of air between his lips
If I am patient, he will move and fold himself toward the moon
    patterned wall

And I his disciple
    can follow
I conform to his body,
My jutting neck realigns to fit
    his downy head under my chin
My spine slowly straightens as I press my chest against his back
Together we form a C
as our legs curve in unison.
My knees serve as the pedestal for his tiny feet.

I listen. I follow.
He breathes.
I breathe.
My heart slows to his steady beat.
I lie in sync
with his slow
        waltz
        time.

STONEWOUNDS

ANNE-MARIE OOMEN
Lake Forest, Illinois

I am hiking a mountain for the first time in my life when I break the tree line and look up to the crest. I am suddenly dizzy and inexplicably afraid. I stop, resting against the granite of New Hampshire's Mount Cardigan. I see the quartz for the first time. Long veins of lighter quartz cross and crisscross the dark granite like a child's script, teasing some words or a story just to the edge of recognition—a mystery, almost a meaning. I hear in the abrupt wind some question that I do not understand. Then, I remember.

On the rocklines of this old mountain, the stone stories are slipping back to me. Stone stories thread through me as quartz through this mountain, but like the shadow that lace casts, the pattern is dark, the holes, filled with light. I begin to climb again, turning my mind away from my anxiety, making an odd preparation to reach the crest. First, I remember only that stones have marked graves for a long time. That, and Isaac.

On the huge fields, swamp, and pastures of the Michigan farm where I grew up, my siblings and I were only forbidden to play on one acre of untilled hillside north of our asparagus fields. An odd Eden. The old Native American chief, Isaac Battice, the man who would later tell me the story, spoke to my father, explained that two generations before my father's father bought the farm, it had been part of a reservation. On the southwest slope of this hill lay a tribal cemetery, probably the first one established in Oceana county after the mission and settlement era. My father agreed to Isaac's request; the cemetery would be left alone. Even his children, who roamed everywhere over the hills, would not play there. Thus, it became one of our favorite haunts. Wooden crosses buttressed our forts; we ransacked the remnants of a fence to make toy guns.

Isaac was one of the few members of the local Potawatomi tribe who had not left. He lived in what we called Shanty Town, a few small, battered shacks down by the big spring. My father kept an eye out for him hitchhiking, and my mother drove down after bad winter storms to see if he was still alive. That was the extent of it. I used to stare at the way he walked, an odd gait that must have covered terrible arthritis. I didn't understand about him being "Indian." Years later, during the growing consciousness of the sixties, I sat in Isaac's shack, intent on interviewing him. We shared a bottle of cheap wine. He stood near a smoking oil furnace in a room that became suffocatingly warm and picked out old church hymns on a three-stringed fiddle. A storm was blowing up from the lake. Thunder fed the oily air.

While the storm built, he told me the stone story. I've lost details, but I remember it like this: Before time began the People fought a great battle. The battle raged over the whole world, and the greatest warriors, warriors with the best skills, finest weapons, and fastest bodies fought in this battle. The battle raged on and on over land and time. The warriors had to fight to the death. And at last, after much time had passed, they all killed each other. But their battle was so great that when they died, these warriors turned to great stones that are marked by lines of lighter horizontal color, like layers between a cake. The legend held such strength that the first missionaries who came to Michigan's coast allowed the Potawatomi to place these rocks in the older cemeteries where the warriors could be honored with the newly dead. But after the second wave, when the missionaries built the new Saint Joseph's mission with its new Indian cemetery, the priests placed the rocks outside this new cemetery and forbid the Potawatomi from touching them because the stones represented a pagan practice. Isaac told me the stones disappeared. Then he laughed and said that at night the tribe moved them back into the older cemetery, the one that would no longer be used, the one priests would forget.

Isaac told me how to know these stones. He showed me the older cemetery—not the one on the farm—in a wooded hillside in Elbridge township. Overgrown, no crosses, and few gravestones survived. One plaque did claim to mark the grave of Chief Cobmoosie, the man who was supposed to have hidden the gold when tribal lands were sold to the government. Here also stood warrior stones like trolls, three to five feet high, squat and slim, tilted with vine. Through the dark rock, slim horizontal lines of a lighter granite or quartz ran like veins. Isaac touched these lines, reminding me, "These are how you will know."

Thousands of miles from my Great Lakes homeland, I touch rock on an old mountain in New Hampshire—granite streaked with foam from Earth's great cool down. Geology, however, does not stun me as much as legend, the sudden thought—how huge, how magnificent were these warriors. It strikes me that I am climbing rock remains of warriors as huge as mountains. Here the battle was so great and fought so hard, warriors died above clouds and became crests of mountains.

My father's huge hands grapple with the wheel of the pickup as he swings onto a two track bordering the asparagus field. It is a spring Saturday, and it is my niece, Brooke's, eighth birthday. I am home, a rare visit. With my sister, Jo, and our father, we are in charge of seven grandchildren. The "silly seven" have piled into the truck bed except for Brooke who rides with us in the cab.

"Why are we going here?" she asks as Dad drives deeper into the farm hills.

"We're looking for an old cemetery," Jo explains.

"How come?" Brooke asks.

"We want to see if we can still find it."

"But why?" Brooke insists.

"People are buried there."

"Can we really find it?"

"We don't know. We used to play there," I sigh. "But we beat it up pretty bad, when we were your age. There may be nothing left."

Dad shakes his head.

"Will there be ghosts?" Brooke's voice, unsure. Jo hugs her only daughter.

"No, Brooke, we want to stake it so you will all know." Jo explains.

"Nothing to be afraid of," this, my dad's voice. "We just want to remember."

"Why do we want to remember?"

"It's a sacred thing." He rumbles softly on, sounding remarkably like an old chief I knew.

He parks the truck, pulls out the shovel, and four long iron stakes. The kids tumble out like puppies, bumping into each other, piling onto the land. Jo calls them before they spread too far, and they come back, tethered to her voice. Dad squats on his heels, knees splayed a little, elbows resting on his knees, huge hands hovering over air and sand, making an odd blessing. His voice quiets as he tells what we are doing. "We're looking for an old cemetery where some people are buried. We're going to mark it. You kids must promise never to till this land." Then he tells them about Isaac and the Potawatomi and the farm.

Jo takes up the narrative. "We want you all to know where it is so you can help each other remember."

Then Dad talks a bit more about what the word sacred means.

A mountain breeze springs up. I move across steep rocks, pushed by this coolness and my memory of a story and an incident that opens my understanding of this mountain. Stories understand what we don't. In the world in which I grew up, when we had awe, or reverence, or fear for what we did not know—even if we couldn't put these words with what we were feeling—we made stories for these feelings. Remembering stories answered questions and eased uncertainty or fear. ("Dark" was Sunshine taking its nap. You could imagine somewhere the Sun curled in a ball and resting, its head tucked in its own golden arms. Once you knew that, you knew the Sun would come back.) My present fear eases. I begin to think what it will be like to step through the lace of these rocks onto the light of a mountain top.

Dad and Jo find the south ridge almost immediately. It ends abruptly on the brow of the southeast view. I ask Dad if he knows what created the ridge. "The earliest farmers who didn't till this acre plowed right up against its boundary. Over generations, their own fields began to wash away. But in here, the cemetery grasses anchored the topsoil in place." We walk the ridge. On the north side of this boundary, wild grapes are dense, coiled into a dark tangle over which the kids trip, whining that these woods are "boogie trapped." Five year old Luke gives Jo an "eye poker," a stick hooked at one end, and informs her that one of the trees "lost it and might need it later." The scrub forest thickens with saplings on which the kids swing. Jo and Dad and I follow the shallow ridge, looking for a clue to the north-south boundary, which will give us then one corner and two sides of the plot. We find the rotted wrist of a cedar pole. The second corner is discovered, but now the ridge has faded. Finally, by

digging on a parallel line to the first ridge, our hands touch on
a line of barbed wire rusted as blood, embedded in leaf mold. It
guides us to the third corner. There, under wood refuse, we find
a large stone. It is a marker stone, as smooth and round as giant's
bone. I realize how difficult it must have been to get it here.
From this point, we estimate a square plot. The last corner fits
when Zach, the oldest boy, digs until he finds termite dust ten
or twelve inches below the surface, wood turned into red powder,
a sign that a cedar post had held this last corner.

As we discover each corner, my father drives in a stake. The
children, wild with wind and fascination, swarm into ritual sponta-
neously as we drive in the last one. They tumble against my father,
grabbing the stake, swinging on this new boundary marker. Suddenly he announces, "Kids, we're gonna walk the boundary again,
all the way around so you won't forget." At each corner each child
places a small hand around the stake and holds it. A silent vow
occurs: "Never forget the boundaries again." We walk this small
plot and at every corner seven children and two sisters and their
father take hold of the iron. It vibrates as three generations of
hands promise to remember a boundary. On the third corner,
where the bone-stone lies, my father has driven the stake outside
the line so that now the stone rests within the cemetery. The children put their hands on the stake, but they also touch the stone,
brushing away dirt as they climb over it. On the way down, Brooke
hangs back, takes her grandfather's hand and says, "This sure was
a funny birthday present, Grandpa."

I take the last strides and at the brink of the mountain, the wind
and view brings a final clarity. I look around at this fine old
mountain warrior and I feel nothing of the conqueror, more the
trespasser, but I am here. I bend down and with my hands I
touch a wide line of running quartz. What Isaac said—these lines
are the wounds of warriors, wounds so great they remain to
mark and remind how they died. I walk over the crest, more
reverent than I ever have been in church, awed at these marks
left by weapons I cannot imagine, tracing a web of stone that
never heals, honoring that death exists and stone is the closest
thing to eternity that we know.

The wounds identify the stones. The warriors did not live to
sing their exploits, but their wounds remain forever to mark the
land. I lie down on the rock. Isaac never told me if their deaths
or the battle were honorable; he only told me that it happened,
how to know and remember. Perhaps the story is a reminder to

be tenacious, to fight to the death; perhaps it is a reminder to keep the peace because the great battle has already been fought, the sacrifice already made. But I think meaning rests in the story itself. We make stories to answer great questions, and good stories last because they mean many things.

I hope my siblings' children will remember not to till an acre of land marked by a stone, bones, and four iron stakes. I hope the story of seven children being taken by two sisters and their father to drive stakes in a hillside will last. If we are very lucky, the story will run ahead of us for as long as the wounds in these mountains. Because these lines—on the page and on the stone and now in your memory—are more than a story to trace with your fingertips, these are the open places, the wounds of making and unmaking meaning.

Today I have climbed a warrior so great that I lie down in the rocklight of a story. My body rests parallel to a wound in stone that is like blood running forever stilled in Isaac's tale. I fall asleep here in light and wind, knowing the great warrior on which I sleep is protected by and linked to the iron stake of story and the stone of memory.

About the Process: One Writer's Wound

Stapled to the back cover of my writer's journal, the one I carry everywhere, the one where I also tuck the most recent set of student essays, a tea-spattered sheet of heavy paper lists family stories. It once hung on my refrigerator because family stories most often surfaced while friends and relatives sat around my kitchen table. I had learned that these important conversations were transient. Unless I found a recall trick, I would forget the memory or story that had delighted me. So, while I brewed the second pot of tea, I'd jot down a phrase or working title to jog my memory. The words "Stone Story—Isaac" had been scrawled down along with a few dozen other equally obscure references on that sheet of paper many years ago. I hoped someday I would find time to write about them all but until then, the prompt would hold the ideas in my memory.

Then, in the spring of last year, my family rediscovered the old cemetery. The incident moved me to write a skeleton version in plain prose. At that time I saw little connection between the stone story and staking the cemetery, certainly not enough to pull together in an essay.

That summer, I began reading Annie Dillard and Gretel

Ehrlich. I noticed they made odd connections. Loops of meaning unified their pieces and, I thought, gave them depth. Though I was a fledgling essayist, making my first forays into creative nonfiction, I admired their work and I, well . . . I wanted to write like they did, write something that made those unexpected and startling associations. I tried a couple of imitations, but the writing was too contrived. From the attempts I deduced that Dillard's and Ehrlich's unity was created from an organic quality, not randomness or cleverness. I sometimes have to stop and remind myself of what I tell my students: The best way to make something out of a failure is to be patient. One way or another failure turns into something else—not always success perhaps—but something else. I put aside my attempts and waited.

A favorite line from William Stafford's *Writing the Australian Crawl* gave me a clue to the organic unity quality I admired in Dillard's and Ehrlich's work. He writes, "a writer is not trying for a product, but accepting sequential signals and adjustments toward an always arriving present. To slight that readiness . . . would be to violate the process, would be to make writing into a craft that neglected its contact with the ground of its distinction." I had been slighting my readiness, focusing too hard on a product. The day that changed, I was hiking a mountain. I experienced a moment of vertigo and had to look down and really concentrate on the rocks to get my balance back. When my husband and I reached the top, I remembered looking at lines in the rocks. I said something like, "Look at these." As our conversation meandered, I told my husband the story about rock lines, the story Isaac had told me. He had heard it before but had never seen an example. We were both a little awed by the association of these lines with the warriors. He suggested the idea was a poem. I agreed it had the mystery with which poetry often begins.

But when I tried to write the poem, it turned out preachy. The idea seemed too informed and the language too prosey. Though I have written enough to know a better craftsperson might have been able to do it, I decided to follow the advice of my much-admired teacher, Bruce Ballenger, and trust the writing to lead me. It was a breakthrough for me to trust the writing more, control it less. I studied the poem draft and remembered the way Dillard tells more than one story at a time. I began writing in prose, without attention to form, simply writing the two parts, the mountain hike and Isaac's story. It was then the organic quality began to assert itself. I discovered I could not write about the story without also writing about cemeteries. The "ground of distinction" came when I let myself wander from the story of the hike into the story of staking the cemetery.

I wrote very quickly after that, forcing myself NOT to think of the whole shape, only the next association, one thought at a time. I realized quickly the piece could not be constructed chronologically, that I would have to deconstruct time a little. Another breakthrough. I was learning that nonfiction might be shaped differently. I allowed the mountain hike to fall away, and simply wrote, alternating between the two stories. When I came to a pause in my thoughts, I picked up on the other part and let the immediacy of the images carry me.

I didn't let the piece rest as I often do but rushed into the drafting process. Usually I spend a lot of time sorting out structure from my zero drafts, but in this case I decided to trust it. Instead, I spent my time doing what Rosemary Deen and Marie Ponsot call "rewriting," that is, working with the sentences, words, the small parts rather than big things, allowing the ideas to fend for themselves. But as I worked with the sentences, the close readings led me to the idea, the center or "thesis" of the piece, a deeply held personal belief that stories are connected to us and connect us in ways that move past the limits of time.

When I was asked to write about my writing process, I felt a pang. I don't think about process much except to be patient with it. Trying to remember and reconstruct the sources and steps frustrated me at first because these things didn't seem important. Through this process essay, I have realized how many new things I tried in "Stonewounds" and how many of them have since become habitual. For the first time I let my reading strongly influence me. I trusted the writing to *lead* me rather than me lead it. I tried what seemed impossible: using different time frames, telling more than one story at a time, and discovering meaning last. I am grateful for the insights.

INSIGHTS INTO COMPOSING THE POEM "WORD RAFT"

SHERRY FALCO
Silver Creek Elementary School
Silver Creek, New York

*C*omposing a piece of writing is an incredibly messy process for me. I guess I think of myself as a builder. My mind is like a construction site, and I construct images from thoughts. A piece of writing develops slowly over time and generally starts with what I call a *brick* or a *block* idea. This initial idea lays around in my mind for a bit while I subconsciously add more and more material to the pile. The brick idea for "Word Raft" was an emotional incident in my personal life. The idea went through many construction changes over several months.

When I was cleaning my mother's attic after she had passed away, I discovered a carefully packed box of airmail letters that my father had sent to her starting in 1943 right after they were married and he had joined the navy. I ran my hand over the tops of the letters. I felt I wasn't ready to discover anything new about my parents at that time. The letters were there, however, and occasionally tugged at my mind so on a hot July day I took them home and began to read them.

As I read, I remember the vivid feeling of disappointment I felt because the letters were so mundane. After awhile that feeling was replaced by a devastating feeling that although I was holding my father's words, I could no longer remember the sound of his voice. It was hard to pull away from the letters, but I went downstairs that day and wrote the following entry in my journal:

> I spent some time in the late afternoon looking at some of the letters my father sent to my mother during the war years. They were quite mundane correspondences relating his day-to-day activities,

44

problems and worries. He was, after all, an uneducated man. In fact, when I think of his early life in West Virginia as a school drop-out and runaway, I guess I'm more impressed than I was at first. He wrote a great deal more, I'm sure, than many men. Because he died when I was fourteen, I've forgotten so much about him. He was a pretty silent person who drank too much. The letters give him a voice I never knew. It's odd because the voice has no auditory connection and yet the handwriting is so familiar. So many times I try to recall him, but the memories are faded. I am now, at forty-two, older than he lived to be. The letters are precious to me.

I then simply moved to the next page and began this poem:

Untitled

The assumption is
you'll remember
forever the faces
the voices of childhood
but today my middle-age
body is perching on
the edge of a bed
struck by words
from my father
a common voice
speaking from forty-six
years in the past.
Boring vignettes from
a sailor not yet in
the war to his wife, my mother
"honey I miss you"
Both gone now I sit
as my mother
reading words from
a face in faded pictures
a voice with no sound
just patterns on paper
these words on a page
so precious I strain
to hear him, know him
touching the words with
my eyes, how lucky
I am to have so
much of him
the precious, precious words.

I left those newly discovered insights and emotions in my journal that day and didn't return to them for four months. At that time, I needed a piece of writing for a one day workshop I was in so I went back and reworked the poem trying to set up white space and line breaks. I shared it with a colleague in a demonstration of conferencing techniques and was stunned at the emotion this quickly drafted effort evoked in the audience. When I finished reading the piece, I saw several people wiping tears from their eyes. After the workshop session, two or three individuals talked to me and related that the poem had evoked images and thoughts of their own parents. One friend said it made her reflect on how we all casually accept the on-going presence of our loved ones seeming to take them for granted until it is too late and they are gone. I thought at the time I had risked too much, let something too close to me be exposed. I had only shared my poetry in public once before and was not prepared to accept that my simple words might have the power to move people as much as this piece had. It took me some time to internalize the fact that through my writing I could invoke images and feelings in people that were not only quite personal but sometimes moving and powerful. Was this a fluke? Could I write like this again? Were my thoughts worthy enough to be read by others? Because of the confusion of feelings that I was experiencing, I filed the poem away along with the memories of the audience reaction and never worked on it again until I went to the University of New Hampshire to participate in the summer writing institute.

I hadn't brought my earlier drafts of the poem with me, but in the atmosphere of a supportive writing community of teachers, I put the letter poem on my list of possible topics.

I surprised myself this time by starting with an idea web. I don't often do this, but I had to smile because it looked just like the ones I show my students how to make. (See Figure 1.)

I then began a new draft remembering the main concepts of a voice I could no longer remember and a feeling that while reading these words, I could actually become my mother and try to feel what she felt all those years ago.

After two or three drafts of just getting my ideas down, I shared the poem with my peer response group and found I needed to clarify the image that I had actually become my mother while reading the letters. Someone in the group commented that the images of water were very relevant and helped tie the themes of the poem together. The response startled me because I didn't consciously intend this. When I finally confer-

Figure 1

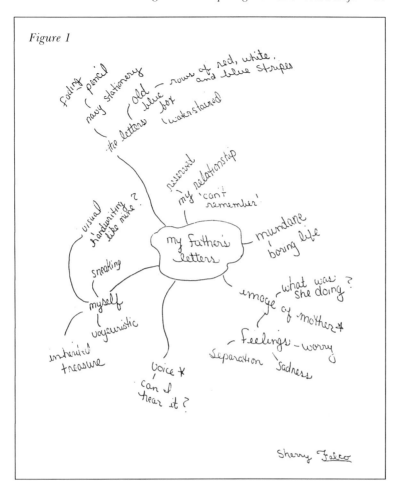

enced with Tom Newkirk, my writing instructor, I had more specific questions to ask. "Are my water images vivid enough and do they connect throughout the piece? Have I shown the tragedy of losing the voices of loved ones?"

Tom felt it wasn't clear at the beginning of the poem that it was my father's voice I was talking about. He also suggested that I put more actual excerpts from the letters into the poem since the piece was, indeed, about my father's voice. I worked through one or two more drafts of major changes before I was fairly satisfied that I had finished. I then spent time fussing and polishing and eventually had to force myself to leave the work alone. Even a year later when I pulled the piece out for a poetry reading, I again made some minor revisions. It's the way I am, I can drive myself crazy doing this.

Reflecting on the way the writing process works for me, I find it's important to keep all of my drafts so I can see the changes I've made. Now as I look at the collection of drafts from my first brick idea for "Word Raft," I'm fascinated to see the struggles and changes that I went through. They are not all explainable. But I know one thing from looking over the drafts: it is critical for me as a writer to get responses. What I think and feel is filtered through the perception of others. I can't know if I am being clear and creating images others can see and feel unless I share work in progress. I think it's important for adults to be in writing groups and to learn to listen honestly and critically to each other. As a writer, most of my brick ideas can be created from small events—something seen, smelled, touched or heard—that, in turn, trigger other memories that may then be built into a complex structure in my mind. Crafting that structure with words is the hard work. As I build, I look to others for honest responses. There are times when I tear down whole structures and start again. There are also times when I create crooked, ugly structures and just walk away and leave them. I know that I want to craft words into structures that are pleasing and/or powerful to the mind's eye and that cause others to build meaningful images and connections of their own. This is when I feel that I have done what a writer should do.

Word Raft

The assumption is
you'll remember forever
the voices of childhood.

Lost for twenty-five
years the voice
of my father floats back

A tattered crew of letters
lined up military style
their red, white, and blue
stripes march in orderly rows
down the length
of the water-stained box.

Airmail missives
long-ago landed
boring, daily vignettes . . .

"It's hotter than blazes here
on the base, but the food's o.k . . ."
from a sailor not yet
in the war to his new wife,
my mother.
"Honey, I miss you."

Now I'm my mother
sitting on the edge
of a bed touching
ship-emblazoned pages
trying to remember
as the words, "I can't
wait to get on the carrier . . ."

Flow into my mind
Turning into waves
on the Lake Erie shore
that pound his hard, skinny
body clad in wool
bathing trunks while
bright sunlight netted in green water
captures my mother's
shore-bound voice

"You're safe, Sher, your father
was a sailor you know."
And the waves swell
the shining surface to reflect
his smile and amplify
his quiet words,

"Go on,
I'm here,
Don't be afraid."

Then sand-shattered surf
pushes me back
reminding me that both
are gone and I
replay again and again
the never-asked question.

The letters . . .
why did she keep them?
Did they save her
from drowning
when he suddenly died?

They're only words
carelessly crafted
in pencil, softening
with time
and memory
a soundless voice,
patterns on paper
frail symbols
on a yellowed page.

I emerge slowly,
painfully from
my mother's body
and damp, fragile,
moth-like
I'm suddenly struck,
wounded by what
I cannot hear.

As I cling to this
small, rectangular
paper life raft
listening, listening
grateful to be
awash in his
precious words.

BRIDGING THE GRAND CANYON

VICKI SWARTZ
Boise-Eliot Elementary School
Portland, Oregon

*T*he five eight- and nine-year-olds sat cross legged on the corner rug. Sheryl presented the third chapter of her fictitious story *Cats are Cool* while Kurtis fiddled with the pop-up art he had created in his new 3-D book. Lonnie read the first part of his story on three brothers whose parents divorced, a plot clearly reflecting the real-life changes and fears in his own family. Tonya had nothing in her hands, having just returned to school after being absent for a week.

Samuel read his revised poem:

> I look at the stream.
> I like it when it's glittering
> and slithering.
> I see trees swaying
> back and forth.
> I see a mountain with
> big candied rocks.
> I feel peaceful.

The yellow sticky note of questions the group had asked about his poem last week was still stuck to his paper, but now had lines boldly drawn through each one.

"How do you like it now?" he asked. Samuel owned that poem, and his words commanded a confidence I hadn't seen all year.

A few years back I would have given a writing assignment cold, sat back as my fluent writers soared and given gentle squeezes of encouragement to the napes of the necks of my struggling less

53

fluent writers. I probably would have accepted anything pro-
duced and doled out heartfelt praise. I realize now that's what I
did well in my fledgling years as a teacher of writing. I encouraged and built up kids' fluency. But their audience was me, and
I taught them how I was pleased. What I didn't do, because I
didn't know how, was help my writers to craft their writing, to
improve it, to revise it, to help them get that feeling of victory
when you know your words finally, at long last, have said just
what you want them to say. What I didn't do was give them
the tools to help improve each others' writing, which eventually
translates into improving their own writing. I had only begun
experimenting with what I was learning about children in their
middle years and their craving for peer approval and contact,
and using it to my advantage in establishing a classroom where
there were twenty-eight writing teachers. No professor had ever
mentioned to me that the comments the students make to one
another hold more weight than mine ever could.

As I revisit the idea of writer's workshop in my classroom and
others, I am reminded that, as Donald Graves (1983) said so long
ago, "Every person has a story to tell." Stories that document our
growth as teachers, that show how we've gone about changing
our teaching practices, how we've let go of old methods, how
we've risked—or avoided risking—in our slow, uneven, sometimes jagged journey toward improved instruction. Stories that
mention the interruptive fire alarms and the messiness of it all.
Stories that don't imply a discovered path or cure-all management system but that instead reflect the hard work and ambiguity
involved in bridging the gaps—okay, canyons—between theory
and instruction.

I offer my story, or at least bits of my story, to show my own
struggle in bringing my actual classroom practices more in line
with the theory of writer's workshop. I'd like to say the near-
religious experience I had a few summers ago called The National Writing Project immediately revolutionized my teaching
of writing. But getting the philosophical underpinning to the
writing process wasn't the whole story, the real story. Things just
don't happen that easily or quickly. Giving my students writing
folders for the first time with room for lists of future topics inside
the front cover does not tell how hard it was for me to let go of
my huge file of story starters—you know, the kind that sidetrack
student minds with a random picture or sentence, as if they
would have nothing to say without our teacher prompts. After
the writing project, I understood the rationale for having

students write mostly on topics of their own. But throwing away this folder, with papers I had spent so much time designing and that had in fact prompted some pretty wonderful student stories in past years, was, well, not so easy to do.

Scheduling daily blocks of time for writer's workshops does not tell how difficult it was for me to deal with those four or five students who wrote so slowly and so painstakingly, or who were pulled out of my classroom so much that when I said, "Choose your favorite piece of work this month to publish!" only had one thing from which to choose. They ended up publishing practically everything they ever wrote, which seemed better than not publishing at all, but wasn't quite right.

Attempting to keep track of twenty-eight chatty planets orbiting around me with neat little checklists and narrative notes does not depict the total classroom management scene. I felt a loss of teacher control when I allowed the students to go through the writing process at their own pace. I panicked that some were slipping through the cracks, looking busy but really not producing much. I feared spending too much time with my more demanding students and not getting around to everyone often enough, especially my quiet kids who slipped neatly behind the bookshelves, their knees drawn up, sandwiching their writing out of my view.

Using the "little blank book" idea I got from one of my team teachers (three to five pages of typing paper folded in half and stapled along the spine, book-style) for my beginning writers to draft their first stories turned out to be less of a Oh-now-I-get-it cure-all than an important way for me to observe how emergent writers develop their sense of story and of books. It was like getting a good refresher course in child development and discovering that older children are more *like* than unlike their former selves. I suddenly better understood my middle-years writers who slipped in and out of stages, sliding up and down on the continuum of growth.

Moving from third to fourth to fifth grade with my same class I experienced great joy in looking at writing development on a horizontal continuum. By comparison, the vertical grade level pieces of curriculum I was handed each successive year were disillusioning. It was as if someone had taken a giant exacto knife and randomly sliced up a list of "everything important to teach" and doled out a strip to each grade level. It seemed so arbitrary and artificial. Too many of my youngsters simply didn't fit the assembly line mold.

Because I stayed with my class for three years and had a chance to see their growth and development as writers and thinkers, I felt a deep disappointment, almost grief, in knowing that they would no longer have writer's workshop the year after they left me. The staff at the next grade level had no background, training, or experience in process writing. With this realization I found myself tempted to shift my position against a strict standardized curriculum. At the time, I sat on a district language arts committee and was exasperated at how students can have entirely different writing experiences from year to year depending in whose classroom they happen to be placed. I also felt confused about whether we should legislate philosophy when I knew the importance of constructing my own blueprints. In the end I held steady to the belief that teachers must be given training and time to implement such practices.

And joining an adult writer's response group, knowing that my skills as a teacher of writer's workshop would only improve with practice in drafting and revising my own personal writing, does not tell the guilt which I felt at the end of so many long days when I had the best of intentions to write, but found myself collapsed in bed instead, exhausted from the pulse and throb of teaching, once again struggling as my work life blurred into my other-life.

Many parts of writer's workshop still perplex me. Publishing student work continues to be a thorn in my side. Managing a publishing house at our elementary school has proven to be more difficult than simply securing equipment, which wasn't easy. Parent volunteers call in sick, or don't show up, or are unable to read some of the rough work my students turn in. When the turnaround time slows, I find myself racing to my computer and mass producing books so that my young students have the immediate feedback they need to keep them going. But who runs the daily writer's response groups while I am wildly word processing? When the children finally taste the glory of publication, I am faced with the challenge of how to keep myself from drowning in the huge stacks of work that need responses. It still takes me *time* to be thoughtful in my responses to students.

I struggle with assessment. I probably keep too much important information in my head. While there are a lot of interesting authentic assessment tools out there, I want to record only what actually influences my instruction and what gives students and parents good information. There was a time in my teaching, not so very long ago, when I looked at assessment as an end product and not as an ongoing process. I have complained about being asked to assess too much and too frequently. It was as if my grade book and clipboard with all the class lists of check marks and data was being kept for someone else and not me or my students (ring any bells for you?). I have merged several other teachers' ideas into an assessment system that still doesn't feel polished. I keep anecdotal notes on what the students are writing and what I think they need to work on. I also have the students set writing goals and conference with them individually to evaluate their growth. Finally, I find myself a manic assessor. I keep all sorts of notes for a while and then drift off entirely, not wanting to be bothered with the upkeep of it all. I humbly acknowledge that my brain gets overloaded and I am not always able to keep the nuances of each child's writing in my head. But I find my teaching is better with the assessment.

I am also concerned about the discrepancy between the practice of teaching writer's workshop (all subjects, actually) and then assigning letter grades at the end of each term. A number of colleagues and I have worked on developing a nongraded report card to replace our current system of letter grades—a system that, incidentally, was never intended to show learning (Swartz, 1983)—that gives better information about student progress. The system is an improvement, but still begs to be revised. I collected report card samples from a number of schools that revealed a great interest in alternatives to grading but few examples truly deviated from traditional letter grades. A 1–5 marking code translates easily into an A–F one; an "Excellent," "Satisfactory," and "Growth Needed" code quickly becomes an A-C-F system, even narrower than the five-point grading scale.

And although I articulate a philosophy of valuing diversity—and genuinely love the rich mix of economic level, cultural background, religion, sex, race, ability, and interests in the students I teach—I find myself yearning to surround myself with like-minded colleagues, especially in the area of writer's workshop. But certainly the notion of homogeneous versus heterogeneous grouping with my youngsters must also apply to groupings of teachers, and I must remind myself I have much to learn from all of my colleagues, even those with different value systems and teaching styles from my own.

I would like to say that I've figured out writer's workshop, but I haven't. This concept continually generates questions, but ironically it is this questioning that makes my teaching better.

ironically it is this questioning that makes my teaching better. While there are philosophical goals for me to aim toward, I know there is no direct path that will lead me there. Teachers have room within the concept to invent and create application alternatives. While I find the challenge invigorating, I struggle at times with feeling comfortable with the constant uncertainty of it all. And finding a few minutes to surface for a gulp of thinking time from the ocean of day to day, minute by minute reaction-and-quick-decision-work my teaching becomes is, well, difficult at best.

More than a cloning of practice or teaching style, I seek a sympathetic climate of administrators and co-workers who can revisit writer's workshop with me who truly understand the complexities of my work, the ambiguities of my practice, and the enormity of my job.

References

Graves, Donald H. Summer 1983. Lecture given at Lewis and Clark College, Portland, OR.

Swartz, Vicki. July, 1983. *Student Evaluation: Grading vs. Non-Grading.* Master's Thesis, Bank Street College of Education, New York, New York.

My Class

KATHLEEN MAHAN
Council Rock School District
Newtown, Pennsylvania

*T*he video—glimpses of a writing workshop—watching, and then really seeing *this* classroom. *Not my* classroom, but *this* classroom. Not my faces, but her faces. Knowing I've read journal articles and books, attended classes and workshops, listened to teachers describe successful examples, always picturing my students in their classrooms.

Always wondering why my classroom didn't look quite as neat and tidy and perfect as theirs always seemed when they'd been teaching it. Always wondering what I was doing wrong. But now, pulling this piece into the puzzle and connecting.

Her classroom, via video, an eighth-grade writing workshop in an upper-middle-class white community. Well dressed students, polite students, L.L. Bean models. Well-scrubbed students, on task students.

Writing. Conferencing.

Teacher asking, listening.

Student responding.

Things working like they're supposed to. I remember . . . sometimes my classroom is like this, too.

My classroom. A seventh-grade writing workshop in a small, economically-strapped, blue-collar community across the river from a city. Most in faded, torn, stained "no names." Thrift store throw aways. Animated students, impulsive students . . . distracted students.

My classroom. "Messier than it should be," I think. "Too many students off task."

Adapted and revised after Nancie Atwell's *In the Middle*. With time to write and to read. Mini lessons. Modeling. Conferencing. Purpose. Trust.

My classroom. What makes it different from what I've just seen? What I've been reading?

Tough kids, city kids, scared kids.
Survivers. Losers. The lost.
From single parent, disfunctional, educated, illiterate, intact, homeless families. No families.

Frustration.

"Why do we have to write more?" she asks. "I already know how to write. Ain't nothin' I'm never gonna need writin' for."

"I know you can write," I say. "You have a lot of important things to tell. I just want you to be able to write things better."

"I ain't never gonna do that though."

"What about when you're a little older?" I ask. "Maybe when you want to get a job in a couple years? Maybe you'll need to be able to write notes or leave directions."

"I ain't never gonna want no job like that."

"What kind of job do you think you'd like to have?"

"I don't want no kind of job. All's I'm gonna do is get me a husband and have me some babies. You don't need no writin' for that."

"But, what if you need two incomes? How many families do you know whose mother doesn't have to work too?" ("Gottcha," I think.)

"My momma don't work. She never go to work. My Daddy done support us. My aunt don't work. No way I'm gonna marry no man who can't support me. You think I'm crazy?"

Why are their expectations so low? Why is failing okay? Or just getting by okay? Or barely passing just enough courses to be promoted, okay?

Why can't they understand why reading and writing and listening and thinking and speaking BETTER is *so* important? Why can't they see that the choices they make now directly influence the kinds of choices they'll be *allowed* to make in the future? Tomorrow . . . In five minutes . . .

A twelve-year-old mother. A twelve-year-old whose mother is twenty-four and becoming a grandmother. A twelve-year-old's great-grandmother, so drunk she doesn't know what's goin' on most of the time. A twelve-year-old long on her own.

Surviving. Existing. Dying . . . slowly.

A twelve-year-old girl. Mother in prison. Dad unknown. Lives with grandparents.

Girl remembers mother drunk, mother's boyfriends.

Boyfriend (1) throws girl into swimming pool.

She can't swim.

Boyfriend (2) swings her too high. He won't stop.

Boyfriend (3) hits her. Mom watches.

Boyfriend (4) drives stoned. Girl is scared. Mom laughs.

A twelve-year-old boy. Homeless. The first day wears Mom's shirt and pants and shoes to school.

Kids laugh. Given handouts.

Wears same jeans to school each day.

Kids notice. Kids laugh.

Boy finds sneakers in trash. Wears them.

Sneakers' previous owner recognizes sneakers. Kids laugh.

A twelve-year-old girl. Quiet. Shy. Tormented. Held at knife point. Parents divorce. Lives with Mom. Misses Dad. Sister anorexic. Brother tries suicide.

Slowly pens glimpses of painful poetry.

Surviving. Sharing. Dreaming.

"Someday I want to be an English teacher."

A twelve-year-old boy. Gifted. Failing.

Parent, teacher, student conference.

Boy. Smooth. Detached. Aloof. Angry. Scared.

Teachers. Concerned. Genuine.

Teachers. Frustrated. Assigning blame.

Mother, "Pardon my French, but I think you'll understand. When we gets home, I'm gonna have to get up your ass again. He knows I don't play games. That usually works for awhile. A week or two. Then it seems to wear off, and he goes back to his old ways. I don't know what to do with you. My other kids don't give me no problem."

A twelve-year-old. Old? Yes.

This is my classroom. One hundred and twenty-five students live here. One hundred and twenty-five stories.

This seems so obvious . . . now.

I look at my classroom. "Too noisy," I think. "This is not productive noise. This is off-task noise. Way off-task. Don't they remember what their task is?"

I ask.

"No," they tell me.

I redirect, "What should you be doing?"

"I don't know."

"Tell me what you think you should be doing."

"We supposed to be doing something? Why we gotta work?"

Frustration. My frustration. Why isn't this working the way it's supposed to? What am I doing wrong?

My students for 46 minutes. I wonder how many have the foggiest idea why they're here. I think, "This is not a priority. This is not even in their top twenty or thirty. Would it make their top fifty or one hundred?"

I decide not to ask. I don't think I really want to know.

Clusters of four desks about the room. Book shelves. Books. An area rug. "I need to get it cleaned." Three girls lie on it. Two are reading. One is writing in her journal. Other students are beginning to get books out. Others are working at looking busy. A cluster of students is talking. A girl gets up, walks toward the bookshelf, hits a boy hard, knocks his books on the floor, and keeps walking.

"Now, why'd you go and do that?" he shouts.

I say, "Please pick up his books. This behavior is unacceptable. Please kee . . ."

"NO!! He hits me, I'm gonna get him back."

"But, he didn't hit you."

"Not now he didn't. But he's been messin' with me all day. I'm gonna get him back."

"You wanta fight?" he says as he gets out of his seat.

"Yea, I'll fight you. I'm not scared."

The second hand finally ticks. Others are involved. No one is on task. It feels like everyone is pushing them forward. Cheering them on . . . like for a team that needs to score with only seconds left in the game.

"Whoa," I say. "Not in here. Let's get this under control. Back in your seats. Both of you."

It's like I haven't spoken. The noise escalates as does the tension in the room. They continue toward each other.

"STOP!" I scream. "NOW!"

They stop. It's over for *now*. For this minute. Maybe for the class period, but clearly it's *not over*. Anger simmers. Looks flair. Plots begin. The class is over. 35 minutes left to go. . . .

I look at my classroom. He's just walked in, and he doesn't seem able to control himself. He seems to be bouncing off the walls. We've talked before. Sometimes if I get to him quickly enough, he can save it.

I wonder about today.

It doesn't look good.

"Okay," I think to myself. "Off-task's okay. Be distracted. Stay off-task. That can be okay for today. I can live with that. But don't distract others." I must have been dreaming. He can't just distract himself. Others are pulled in. Some seem too willing.

"I need for you to write in your journal," I say to him quietly. "It seems like you're having a rough time today, but I'd like to see you *really* try to get it together."

"I will," he says. He smiles.

He doesn't.

I ask again.

He doesn't.

I suggest maybe moving to another seat might be a good idea.

He explodes! "Why you always pickin' on me? Why you always asking me to move? Why you don't ask nobody else to move?"

I say to him calmly and quietly, "You either have the choice of sitting where you are and working, moving to another seat and working, or I'm going to ask you to leave. Those are your options."

"Fuck you!" He yells. Class is over. 40 minutes before the bell agrees.

The unpredictable cadence. The rhythm of uncertainty. Escalating tension. Diffusing tautness. Accepting this reality, acknowledging this challenge. Rendering no excuse.

A student asks, "Can we read today?" I look up, connecting voice to face. I'll have to remember this moment.

"What are you reading?" I ask.

"*Dogsong*," he says. "Mike said it was good." His first book not selected by length.

"It just takes time," I think. I must remember to be patient.

This is my classroom with students I've come to know and love. All with needs. Students I must fight for. "Messier than it's supposed to be, and that's okay. Learning isn't tidy."

Crossing Boundaries:
VOICES FROM THE INNER CITY

JOANN PORTALUPI CURTIS
University of New Hampshire
Durham, New Hampshire

DAWN HARRIS MARTINE,
PS 123, School District 5
New York City

ISOKE NIA
Teachers College Writing Project
New York City

*B*oundaries. They are everywhere. Step into the classroom and you are confronted with a boundary that divides adult culture from child culture, school life from home life, and the image of teaching you bring to your work and the classroom you are able to create. Teachers constantly negotiate boundaries. Although no teacher contract spells out the specifics of such border work, an essential skill of teaching is recognizing when a boundary exists and learning to negotiate it.

Ten years ago I left a rural classroom in New Hampshire for a position as staff developer at the Teachers College Writing Project in New York City. I did not know my biggest challenge would be to identify and shuttle between the numerous boundaries separating my familiar world from this new one: the world of white, rural, middle-class school children and the world of poor, minority, urban school children, the world of staff developer and the world of teacher. The work was difficult. I wondered why the writing process model we were using was failing for kindergarten children in a poor district with high minority populations. Although I shared this question with my colleagues at Teachers College, five years later when I left my role as staff developer the question was still unanswered. I had identified the problem, but I hadn't a glimpse of how to understand and solve it.

I am indebted to the work of Lisa Delpit for helping me return to my original question and for offering hope that we may indeed cross seemingly impenetrable boundaries. Delpit's writing points to the missing voices in the dialogue over how best to educate poor children and children of color. She argues that those who hold the power in our culture—mainly white, middle-and upper-class populations, need to initiate dialogue with those who have been silenced. We can not afford to bypass their experience and understandings. Delpit (1988) writes:

> *We must be vulnerable enough to allow our world to turn upside down in order to allow the realities of others to edge themselves into our consciousness. Teachers are in an ideal position to play this role, to attempt to get all of the issues on the table in order to initiate true dialogue. This can only be done, however, by seeking out those whose perspective may differ most, by learning to give their words complete attention. . . .* (p. 297)

Delpit's was the first African-American voice I had heard discussing the value of writing process pedagogy for poor, minority children. She contends that writing process classrooms are better suited for white, middle-and upper-class students. Students from outside those cultures suffer from what she sees as a cultural mismatch. Delpit sees the writing process concept as employing nondirective teaching and shared responsibilities between teacher and student. This method may present problems for students who come from cultures where the modus operandi are explicit language and a more traditional authoritative stance. She questions whether the writing process methodology will teach minority students the skills they need to operate in the culture holding power in our society. She contends these students need more direct teaching consistent with their cultural background.

Her call for more dialogue is valid. I took her advice and phoned two of my African-American colleagues in New York City. I asked if they would talk with me about my question, about Delpit's critique of the writing process concept, and their own experiences as educators of color implementing this philosophy.

On a clear spring day I left my home in New Hampshire and drove the five hour trip that brought me back into the heart of Harlem. Dawn Harris Martine and Isoke Nia were waiting for me on the second floor of Dawn's brownstone in Harlem. At the time of our conversation Dawn was a second-grade teacher in District 5 in Harlem. She now works as full-time staff developer on the staff of her school. Isoke was serving as staff developer in District 17, Brooklyn, and has more recently become a staff developer for the Teachers College Writing Project. Inside Dawn's home I was met with the steamy, sweet smells of down-home cooking. She had prepared chicken, collard greens, and sweet potatoes whipped and seasoned like I had never tasted before. As we sat around Dawn's dining room table eating our meal, we began our dialogue. Reading Delpit I found it easy to believe she was speaking for the African-American community. But Dawn's and Isoke's insights from the urban classroom complicate her argument. They understand what Delpit writes about. But they also believe strongly in the process approach to teaching writing and are cautious about throwing the metaphorical baby out with the bath water. They aren't willing to abandon writing process because of the cultural mismatch Delpit talks about.

On Explicit and Implicit Discourse

Delpit says writing process classrooms rely heavily on the use of implicit language. Research has shown that many poor children and children of color come from homes in which they are familiar with a more explicit language—a language of command rather than a language of invitation. This leads Delpit to suggest that writing process educators be more explicit in their teaching of poor children and children of color. Dawn and Isoke agree with the assertion that their children come to school more comfortable with an explicit discourse, but they believe strongly that their students be able to handle both. This adds a particular dynamic to their teaching.

ISOKE: *I agree there exists a group with the power and a group without the power. I also agree that the group without the power is constantly seeking to get it in many ways that are unacceptable. I want my students to know both. I know that I can go and hang on the corner of Fulton Street, and I can just be right-on-in-it* (Her voice carries the cadence of street language.) *And then I can stand in front of Columbia University, and I can be* **right-on-in-it.** *And I know the difference. I don't think I'm willing to give up saying, "Would you like to do this?" because that is what I really want to say. I want to invite you in. I want you to be able, the learners in front of me, to answer that implicit question. I don't want to say to you, "Today we're going to do. . . ."*

I do it with my own children at home. My daughter, she says to me, "Ma, why do you ask me if I want to go to the store if you're going to tell me to go to the store anyway?" (Laughs) *Okay? And I'm doing that for a reason. I want her to be familiar with the language she's going to face outside of this little circle called her own personal community, her own place where she does have power speaking whatever way she does, and be able to face the real world. I don't want to say, "Okay," and give up. I want to keep doing it and I think that in time we'll get it.*

Dawn brings in the complication created when a staff developer, a white woman who values indirect language, is present at a time when direct language is called for.

DAWN: *Okay, but supposing you've walked into this classroom, and they're all running around screaming at the top of their lungs, and the teacher's standing there in front of the classroom with this outside person, and she's feeling like, Oh my God, you know? And she wants to settle them down to the point where she's saying, "Can we all go to the rug and can we all sit down?" And they're going* (arms spread to signify chaos). *At some point in time you've got to say, "Okay, go to the rug, get your partner and* **sit down**.*"*

ISOKE: *Yeah. I agree if they're running all over the place that I would say, "Get over here on the rug." I sat down night before last and thought about things I actually say in real life classrooms to real life children, and I say things like,* (readjusting her body to lean forward authoritatively) *"If you tear a page out of your notebook I will break your arm."* (Isoke quickly breaks into a rich laugh.) *My children, if you asked them to quote me, they would all tell you that Ms. Nia has said that "If you tear another page out of your notebook I will break your arm. Do you understand that? You are going to take that notebook over there on the rug, and you had better write something* **now**.*"*

JOANN: *There's nothing implicit in that!*

ISOKE: *Yes, that's what I'm saying. That is super duper, absolutely, positively direct, I want you to do it right this minute. I don't have time to play with you, and it better be finished. And there better be writing on the page.*

DAWN: *But once you have that. Once you have that understanding with them that's when you say, "Okay it's time to settle down. It's time to do x, y, and z, and they fall into that."*

On Culturally Defined Authority

Language used in the classroom sends signals to students about the nature of authority in operation. If students come from a culture where authority is demonstrated by directives, the meaning couched in nonexplicit language such as, "Can we all go to the rug and sit down?" might get misinterpreted. Dawn and Isoke acknowledge the tension and respond to it as that—a tension that needs to be understood and explained.

ISOKE: *Well, yes we are raised more authoritatively. We are the ones that got the spankings and the beatings, and we are a more authoritarian people in our households. And we have to be. That's the other thing. In this culture we* have *to be. We have to be able to pull our children back just like this.* (She gestures with a tight fist drawn to her body.) *Because we* have *to. As a mother, I know I have to. I cannot say to my son, "Ah, the sky is beautiful, life is beautiful, just skip and hop along." Because if your son and my son were walking down the same street and something happened, something* different *would happen to* my *son.*

So I understand why it's authoritarian with Black teachers. But I want you to understand that within a classroom setting my children can still get the softness. They can get both. But they have to understand that to get the other one they have to be able to come back to me like this (same gesture). *Okay? That tight. You have to be that tight with them. It's not all flowers and daisies and sunshine. And that has to do with our culture. That has to do with our past here in this country. But I don't want you telling me that I must do this skill's thing with my Black children because they need it. I must do this skill's thing with any child that needs. With* any *child, Black, White, green, yellow, red eyes, orange eyes, whatever kind you want to use it, any terms you want to put it in, bad terms, good terms, you know, slang. You must do this thing, this flexibility, this meshing of the two with* any *child so I'm not willing to say I must do this thing just for the Black child. You must do it with any child.*

Isoke acknowledges the gap between the school experience of many Black teachers and the progressive philosophy that shifts the focus from teacher to student. This shift may be difficult for teachers, but it should not negate the potential effectiveness of this method for Black children. Isoke does not see the writing process concept as a pedagogical mismatch.

ISOKE: *When I do workshops with my teachers, when I go to places where there's only Black teachers, I tell them I'm talking about my* (Black) *children. When I go to talk to teachers of your* (White) *children I can say the same message. I just leave out the word Black.* (Laughing) *Same speech, same words, just cross out the word Black. Every time I get to Black I just leave that word out. I'm serious. The message is the same. I just take out the word Black.*

On Loving the Child

Dawn began employing the writing process model after observing two school colleagues using it successfully with their Black students. In these humanistic classrooms, she saw teachers successfully teaching children the skills needed to function in the culture of power without sacrificing what Dawn and Isoke spoke of as "loving the child."

ISOKE: *People are not loving them. They're not planning special things for them. They're not hugging them. They're not pulling them in close because they're* **them.** *They're rough and they're bad.*

I think you can't stop doing that because our kids come from a culture where everything is hard. Everything is cut to the quick. Everything is rough. You have to cut it to the quick, but I'm going to love you too. I love you, and I'm going to hug you. That's super important. I think of Tiesha who's fourteen years old and in the fifth grade and the last time she took a test she scored something like a 3.5. She's so full of anger and hate and I'll-kick-your-butt. It's important for me to hug, and she doesn't want me to touch her. "Get your hands offa me!" And you know that. (She turns to speak to Dawn) *And you get them in the second grade, "Get your hands offa me." Now that's in second grade—who doesn't want to be hugged!*

DAWN: *When you reach out to cup a face, squeeze a face, they duck.*

ISOKE: *Ducking and they're dodging and then there's—Don't be White! It's hard enough for me to hug them but then if some White teacher tries to hug them they would step back another fifty feet. I don't want you to think that they only step back for you though. They step back for me twenty five, and they step back another twenty five when you try to hug them. That's what I mean. So I think that you can't leave out the humanistic side. You have to pull those children in. Let them know they are loved.*

DAWN: *But you have to know them first. You love all of them, but you can not do the same thing to one that, you know, some kids you absolutely can't hug. Andre, when I go to hug Andre, Andre gets stiff as a board. His eyes bug out of his head and as soon as you turn him loose he runs across the room to do something awful to someone else. What I'm saying is I have to know that although what I'm calling for—what my head is telling me to do—is to reach out and grab him and hold on to him. I know that given that hugging that he responds like eyes rolling back in head, stiff as a board and then runs to the other side of the room and punches the first kid he can find. So I have to give him his hugs in a different way. I have to stand as close as I can possibly stand to him and say good things to him.*

ISOKE: *You're working up to hugging.*

DAWN: *I know not to hug him.*

ISOKE: *But you didn't know him when you got him. You tried to hug him. See what I'm saying? So I'm saying she came in with her **humanistic** self, okay? Hugging Andre. **Hugged** Andre and found out that he's going to have a negative reaction to hugging. So then in her **flexible** self, stepped back and planned how to hug Andre. (Laughter) That's what she did! 'Cause the bottom line of all of that is she didn't stop hugging him. But she figured out how to hug him. She didn't know him when she started that hugging process. She came in her room wanting to hug and love those children. And most people don't walk into a room wanting to hug and love them.*

Love and time figure prominently in open-minded responsive teaching—teaching that is a process of coming to know the child moment by moment, day by day.

DAWN: *Good teaching means knowing the learner. You could be the best teacher in the world and if you start feeling that you know how to teach then you miss some very important things because the kids will teach you how to teach them. The Maori children, the children in the Kamehameha school in Hawaii, the inner city kids will teach you how to teach them. It's meeting them, assessing what it is that they know, bringing them from where they are to someplace else. There are twenty-eight children in my second-grade classroom, and there are twenty-two different cultures, twenty-two different views on literacy. If you look at them they are Black and Hispanic. But in that Black and Hispanic we have children from Santa Domingo, Belize, Puerto Rico, Zaire, and each one of those have different cultures and their views of literacy and reading are totally different.*

Responsive teaching is a way to navigate the often choppy waters that arise when cultural mismatches occur. Learning to navigate is the answer, not the impossible task of steering a course that avoids cultural mismatches altogether. This view of teaching offers a model for teachers to reach children from cultures other than their own.

ISOKE: *I do think you need to know the kids. I don't think that because you're from some other culture that it's hard. I think that I use the word knowing the kids in a different way than Dawn says knowing the kids. When I talk about knowing the kids I may not know anything about their culture. Or learn anything about their culture, though I'd like to. If I remain open when you're learning something I can still help you without knowing your culture. By knowing that whatever I* *just did you didn't get it somehow so I have to do it another way. I have to be flexible enough to change the way I've done it. I think when we make statements about having to know the learner and more about his culture, it leaves out too many people, and it sets up the argument of needing to find folks that match that culture. There are too many people that look like those folks that don't know any more about them than you know. When I've had this discussion with Black educators their position is this: they don't know anymore about that Black child whose father and mother may be on drugs than you do. I think you need to let him know that whatever his culture is, it may not be the one you understand, it may not be the same one you're in, but it **exists**. It's valid for him because he's in the middle of it. You can't say to him, "People don't do that." when he knows that every week they do right down the block from him.*

On Time

Dawn and Isoke are aware that tough inner-city schools often receive less time and resources than more affluent, suburban districts. In response to the question, "What would you do differently in designing an inner-city writing project for the population with which you work?", the answer was straightforward and simple. Give it more time.

ISOKE: *I hold to the fact that I don't think it's been done to the extent that it's been done other places and to the length of time. I think it does need more time. If you thought it took two years or three years for children in that white, middle-class neighborhood then I'd give them five. Okay? And that's truly a thing, if someone said what would I do differently for Black kids or those kids I would give it more time. I'd give it more time because their teachers are less willing to try new things. They are because they get less support or none at all.*

When Isoke worked as a staff developer in one of the largest districts in New York City, she was the only such person on staff at the district office. This contrasts with other, smaller districts in the City where teams of staff developers can work together.

ISOKE: *I go to three schools. They're trying to add a fourth. I'm telling them how crazy they are 'cause I will not do that. I touch thirteen to fourteen teachers. In one of the largest districts in the city of New York. I touch thirteen to fourteen a year. I lose two or three who say, "Oh no, I can't do this." And I keep some. But I'm trying to make [the district office] understand that I've got to make some more of those people hear because the voice that's going to be heard about this is going to have to be the voice of the people who are immersed in this. It really is not going to be that other voice, and it's not only going to be this voice* (referring to Delpit). *She's too far away already. I'm not sure she stayed in the trenches long enough. She didn't stay in the classroom long enough. You have to really stay there.*

*I walk past our classrooms in the morning, and instead of hearing Dawn reading a story—I want her in Brooklyn reading a story—instead of hearing some beautiful voice coming out I hear phonics lessons: eh eh eh eh, ooh ooh ooh ooh, uuh uuh uuh uuh, eeh eeh eeh eeh, ooo ooo ooo ooo. Are these children in pain? **I'm** in pain. Instead of hearing wonderful stories as I pass I hear these sounds. So they don't believe. This is Black people. My superintendent is Black, my assistant superintendent is Black, my principal is Black, the children are Black, the teachers are Black. It's not about being Black here.*

JOANN: *They don't believe and Delpit's articles just fuel their resistance?*

ISOKE: *Yeah. So I'm not willing to say this out loud even though I'm kind of agreeing with you a little bit. I'm not willing to say this—that we need more explicit direction—out loud yet.* **Yet.** *It's too soon to say this. We haven't done writing process enough to say this. Most of us are still doing eee, eee, eee, aaa, aaa, aaa, ooo, ooo, ooo.*

Delpit says you've got to do both so okay we'll do our variation of that and see, that's the problem. They won't go all the way. They won't get the passion. They won't love books. They won't invest in the literature.

It is more common for districts to dabble in a variety of approaches. It's easier to make the initial attempts of importing a philosophy. Districts purchase books. Teachers receive introductory workshops. For some districts that's enough to say they've "got it." But Isoke points out the danger of stopping short.

ISOKE: *And nothing else changes. No schedule changes. No periods made longer and nothing else changes. None of the **other** things that you need to make this process work. You know how many changes— say a school where it's still working—how many changes they have to make in their life in school for this to continue. Ask Laurie Pessah.* (Vice Principal of one of the Writing Project model schools) *She had to make periods longer, give teachers leeway, clean out some rooms, get extra subs. Look at how many changes they had to make for it to work in the place where it does work.*

The experiences of Dawn and Isoke seem to corroborate, at least in part, Delpit's argument that the writing process model can not be blindly transplanted into the culture of inner-city schools. It seems crucial that voices from minority cultures be included in the dialogue of how to adapt an approach like the writing process to the particular needs of urban schools. The voices here suggest that the principles guiding a process pedagogy can find a fresh shape in the context of a new culture. The goals needn't change just as they remained the same in the story of hugging Andre. But it will take time, because it requires the diligence of many teachers for whom this philosophy is foreign and uncomfortable.

ISOKE: *This is what I mean about breaking rules—I told my district I would not work with a class in any school that was less than an hour long. I would not come in there. I wouldn't walk in the door. So in my building, my classes are ninety minutes long—in the other buildings they are an hour long. But in my building they are ninety minutes long, and the teacher and the class come to me 'cause I have a room in my building—and for forty-five of the ninety minutes **another** teacher comes in. Now, when do our children get to work with three adults? Here are three teachers in the room, thirty kids, ninety minutes working on something. See we haven't **done** this. I'm not willing to say let's try both (student-centered process pedagogy and curriculum-driven direct instruction) even though I know, down the line, twenty years from now, I'll be willing to say this. I'll hold this article up and say, "You were right!" But I'm not willing to say it now. Now I want it to still be a secret. It needs to still be a secret because I want you to **do** the other thing. I want you to give as much energy to this new thing, this writing process, this humanistic teaching, this whole language, this loving the children, this whatever you want to call it, implicit language, what**ever** you want to call it, I want you to give the same energy to that you gave to basal readers. That you **gave** to lining them up in straight lines. That you **gave** to hanging the rules on the wall. I want you to **give** the same energy to that, and then I'll let you say this.*

Dawn and Isoke suggest a deceptively simple response to Delpit's argument. If you're trying the writing process model and it's a struggle, don't give up. Don't use culture as a barrier. Just give it more time. Driving home I was full of Dawn's good cooking and the rich conversation she and Isoke had served up after dinner. And I was thankful for Delpit's direction. She is right, there are too many voices that never get heard. If we position ourselves to listen to voices like Isoke's and Dawn's, we can begin to address the fundamental issue of whose voice gets heard. We can have circles of conversation—conversation among colleagues, between teachers and administrators, between teachers and parents, between teachers and their students in any classroom, university to elementary school. We need these conversations if we are to succeed at the hard work of educating other people's children.

Reference

Delpit, L. D. 1988. "The Silenced Dialogue: Power and Pedagogy in Educating Other People's Children." *Harvard Educational Review*, 58(3): 280–298.

NEW QUESTIONS/
NEW DIRECTIONS

HOW PORTFOLIOS EMPOWER PROCESS TEACHING AND LEARNING

SHERRY SEALE SWAIN
Overstreet Elementary School
Starkville, Mississippi

"Gather all your writing, all the things that are in your writing folder or posted on the wall, anything you have published or that you are still working on. Spread it before you. Now try to choose one piece that shows you are a good writer."

It's portfolio selection day, and my first graders recognize these instructions as one of the learning processes of our classroom. A passion for observing developing literacy led me to design a portfolio project to reveal growth in reading and writing over time, so four times during the year my students collect all their writing, published and in-process, and choose one as their best piece. (Four similar selections from their reading workshop journal entries show that they are becoming better readers, but for this article I will confine my story to what happens with the writing only.)

After the students write reflective pieces explaining what their selections show about their writing abilities, the written reflections are attached to copies of the selected pieces of writing and placed in the students' portfolios. The portfolios are thinner, neater than writing folders and insure student awareness and ownership of learning. More on that later.

Selecting pieces for the portfolios requires time for talking and sorting and explaining and responding to preferences. Usually, most of my students have five or six items to choose from, although some have only two or three. If you were to walk into the classroom during this process, you'd notice most of the children standing somewhere near their desks, sharing piles of work with friends.

"Look, I have five: two fact, two fiction, and one riddle book. Are riddles fact or fiction?"

"Hey, we both made pop-up books. Mine is like Eric Carle's."

"That's funny when you made him say, 'In your face!' "

"Help me decide. I like my research book, but my group likes my personal narrative."

Criteria for selections are never posted on a chart or directed with predetermined questions. They emerge from a student's internalized sense of what makes good writing. Kelly says, "I chose my *Cotton* book because I like the way I used a narrator in it, sort of like *The Big Hungry Bear and the Red Ripe Strawberry.* But really I have a double narrator. One asks questions and the other one answers them."

Bonn grins, "I tried to use interesting words in this one like *appeared* and *tumbled* and *scrambled* and *crawled.*"

I follow up by inviting others to learn from Kelly and Bonn, "Did anyone else choose a book with a narrator? a book with interesting words?" What one student expresses gives clues to what others are ready to learn. After listening to Bonn talk about interesting words, Roger re-examines his selection, a book that has resulted from his animal research on snakes. He revises again (although the book was published days ago), adding words and phrases he thinks are interesting: *coiled up like a ball and a crayola* and *poisoned.* All I have to do is spotlight individual learning and invite others to enter into it. Those who are ready, do. Those who are not ready for one concept pick up on another. Samantha selects a draft that contains pages describing what she likes about school and several pages about going camping. She doesn't connect with Kelly's and Bonn's criteria, but when she hears Daniel say that his book is about just one thing, she begins to sort her pages into two separate books. She has the criteria she needs for now; there will be many more opportunities for focusing on narrators and vivid verbs.

Whatever their criteria at a given time, the selection process takes the students back into their writing. Murphy and Smith (1991) contend that the selection process forces students to distance themselves from the piece, to view it as an artifact, a symbol that represents who they are as writers on that day, in that moment of their growth. Selecting becomes part of the learning process.

Reflecting on the selections also requires time, but, without it, we have no portfolio, just a collection of writing. "Look carefully at your choice," I advise. "Think about all the reasons you chose it." Sometimes partners orally share and explain how the chosen pieces show they are good writers. Sometimes we sit cross-legged in a circle on the rug, each person revealing his or her selection and the values attached to it. Mary Beth shares a green poster of an ocean scene with a four-line sentence written in her unique style across the top. On the left side of the poster are photographs and small bits of paper secured by single pieces of tape. She lifts the bits of paper, showing more text underneath, "I picked this one because it shows I can make a double peek-a-boo." The circle disintegrates as her classmates crawl across the rug for a better look.

"How did you do that?"

"Hey, I'm gonna try that in my next book. I bet I can make three peek-a-boos!"

Back at their desks, selected pieces before them, students write their reflections. "At the top of your paper, write the word *Reflections*," I say, writing it on chart paper for them to copy. "Then write to explain to yourself, to your classmates, to me, and to other teachers who may want to read your portfolio, how your selection shows that you are a good writer. Remember all the reasons you chose it. Remember everything your friends said about it. Remember what you said to your partner or in the circle." I encourage volume as they write the reflections because I believe that writing is generative, that the more you write the more you discover and understand what you know. I am quite willing to read the same thoughts expressed over and over as students struggle for an insight that can come only after much mulling of the obvious. When some students seem to have run out of steam, I usually say, "Now turn through your book, page by page. Write about all the wonderful things you did in it."

Like I said, I go for volume. But I don't always get it. Nor do my students always write what I consider to be quality reflections. In October for the first selection/reflection process, twelve of the seventeen students who wrote reflections selected pieces because they valued the mechanics of their handwriting! I was crushed. I had not emphasized letter formation or even neatness. My students had learned to draw letters of the alphabet out of a need to write poems, stories, thoughts. Not once had we practiced making line after line of balls and sticks. I consoled myself with the thought that, as a baseline, at least these reflections were guaranteed to reveal growth in the end!

For her first selection, Jennifer chose a poster she'd made in response to my reading of *Ramona the Brave* by Beverly Cleary.

Daniel chose a book he'd made as a result of our cotton study. Their reflections are shown here:

Jennifer
    Poster based on
    Ramona the Brave
I picked this because we read Ramona. Ramona had to go to the front of the room. It was my best handwriting.

Daniel
    Cotton
I picked this because I put question marks and I put flaps.

[Daniel had written additional text under each of his "flaps."]

It was January before we selected pieces of writing again. While most of the October responses had been one or two sentences in length, these were longer, ranging from a half to a full page. This time only three of the fifteen students who wrote reflections mentioned mechanics. Nine talked about the content of their pieces; eight referred to their writing processes; nine pointed out elements of style; one called attention to response from another class member and one referred to illustration. Jennifer's and Daniel's responses read:

Jennifer
    Jennifer's Family
This shows I am a good writer because it is my best book. I like the book because I like when my baby doll said, "This is fun." I like my characters. They are a baby doll, a gray dog, a dad, a mom.

Daniel
    The Monsters in My Dreams
I picked this because it is a long book. I put who the characters are. I wrote all about one thing, and I kept on adding words until it was just right.

By March when we wrote the third reflections, many of the twenty-one responding students filled a notebook page with thoughts about their writing. Fifteen reflected on elements of style they had learned; fifteen recognized the value of their content; ten called attention to their writing processes; six wrote about revising. One student mentioned response from another class member, and one referred to illustration. Jennifer, having made revisions to it, chose *Jennifer's Family* again while Daniel chose a wordless book by Ezra Jack Keats to which he and his friend Bonn had added text. Jennifer and Daniel were the only two students who mentioned mechanics in their reflections.

Jennifer
Jennifer's Family

This book shows I am a good writer because I put talking on the first page and on the last page. I put periods on every page. I put people's names on pages 2, 3, 4. I put funny stuff on pages 4, 5, 6. I went back and added other words on pages 2, 3, 6. I put long sentences on pages 2 and 6. My book is about my family. I picked this book because my family is the best.

Daniel
Skates

This book shows I am a good writer because I wrote action. Look on pages 1, 3, 4, 5, 6, 8, 9, 10, 11, and 13 where I put action in. I put commas, conversation bubbles, apostrophes, and quotation marks. I made long sentences. I filled the page. I put crashing words on pages 3, 5, 7, and 14. I changed some words that I didn't like. I put words that the dogs said when they got hurt on pages 5, 9, and 11. I named the dogs weird names.

And I wrote a lot on this paper that shows I am a good writer.

By May none of the twenty-four students who participated in the selection/reflection process mentioned mechanics. Seventeen called attention to style, thirteen to content and process; eight described response; six discussed revision; and six commented on illustration. Jennifer selected a personal narrative about her struggle to learn to feed her family's fish. Daniel chose a lengthy piece of fiction that had been through numerous revisions.

Jennifer
Fishyfoo

This book shows I am a good writer because it was about when I was young. What did you like about my book? I put talking. I put names of people. I put pictures. I put a big word. It was *just **popped** in the kitchen.* Jamie helped me figure out to put in *Just when Kelly left* instead of just putting *My sister spended a night with Mandy. I fed too much food, then they died that night.* Then I put that just after (the word) Mandy. I put *Just when Kelly left.* I put a picture on the first page.

Daniel
Secrets of the Ninja

I think this is my best book because I used dialect. I used a bigger binder than I did in any of my books. I worked on it for a long time. I put a lot of words. I was careful with my pictures. I made four pages without any words and I decided to stop drawing pictures until I got more words in. I named all my characters, even me. I used interesting words. I did a dedication page. I colored my pictures. I spelled my name, my mom's name and my dad's name backwards for some

Jennifer
Fishyfoo
The name of this book is *Fishyfoo.* [Jennifer's original sentences read: *My sister spended a night with Mandy. I fed too much food, then they died that night.* Her revision reads: *My sister spended a night with Mandy. Just when Kelly left, I fed too much food, then they died that night.*]

Daniel
Secrets of the Ninja
monsters' names. I tried to model a page sounding like one in *Charlotte's Web.*

Each time students chose pieces for their portfolios, their personal selection criteria seemed to become more sophisticated, and I was sure that the increased fluency of their reflections represented internalized appreciation for their growth as writers. The portfolios were empowering writing process for my students! I made sure the classroom procedures allowed them to be aware of each other's criteria before, during, and after the selection process. The environment was rich with opportunities, expectations even, to learn from each other. The notion of learning in a portfolio classroom is not a foggy, nebulous concept. Learning is concrete, and portfolios offer concrete evidence. Jennifer's and Daniel's reflections show a typical increase in fluency and increasing sophistication. The chart in Figure 1 shows a progression of the entire class. (The variations in the numbers of students responding are due to students transferring in and out of the class, a long illness, and ESL students becoming more fluent in English.)

Figure 1

Components of Reflections	October Reflections (17 students)	January Reflections (15 students)	March Reflections (21 students)	May Reflections (24 students)
Mechanics	12	3	2	0
Content	1	9	15	13
Process	3	8	10	13
Revision	0	0	6	6
Response	1	1	1	8
Illustration	1	1	1	6
Style	2	9	15	17

Portfolios close the gap often left open when we follow the maxim: Children learn by doing. They do, but the doing itself is not the key. To paraphrase John Dewey (1916), we must not only have our students involved in the doing, they must also observe themselves in the doing, and reflect on their observations. In a writing-based classroom, the doing is writing, observing, drawing, moving, experimenting, manipulating, dramatizing, reading, rewriting, seeking response to writing, revising, rethinking, adding to, taking out, writing for oneself, writing for publication, writing for the joy of seeing words dance across the page, writing.

In a writing community, students talk and write to observe themselves as writers. They talk about their writing in whole-class sharing circles and in intimate response groups. Frequently during our writing workshops, a writer will ask groups of two to four students to gather on the rug to respond to his or her draft. They sit in tight circles, eyes intent on the writer as she reads. "What do you like about my book?" she'll ask, expecting a detailed answer from each responder. And detailed answers flow. My students have learned from experience that general compliments (I like your whole book) are not helpful to the writer. Sometimes the responders want a closer look at certain pages; sometimes they ask to hear the book again; often they break off into a discussion of how the writer's book reminds them of a personal experience or of another book. They notice when a friend has worked out a complicated plot. They notice elements of style and compliment effective use of dialogue and metaphor. Then the writer asks, "What would make my book better?" Her responders again make specific comments that lead to improvements:

"I don't understand the part about the talking mermaid doll gift. On the other page, it sounded like you already had one."

"Shouldn't the page about coming down the stairs go before the page about opening presents?"

"You could write a dedication page to your dad since the story is about him."

In my class, students also come every few days for writing conferences with me. "What have you done so far?" I ask and Daniel describes his process of illustrating about four pages at a time, then writing text for those before proceeding. Then he reads his draft, and I compliment the complex plot he has begun. "Have you tried anything new in this piece?" I ask and he explains the dialect he has written for one of the characters. He is especially proud of a page he has modeled after one in *Charlotte's Web*. We celebrate by briefly sharing it with the rest of the class. Daniel's book is wonderful, but I have some honest questions about the content. "Help me understand how the crystal ball fits into the story," I say. "I don't understand how it suddenly appeared." Daniel explains the significance of the ball and tells how he will infuse that information into his book. "What do you need to do next?" I ask to help him set goals at the end of the conference. Later when Daniel chooses this book for his portfolio, he cements his observations in writing.

I've described a hefty investment of instructional time for talking and writing about learning. Observing themselves as writers is important to students' awareness of their own learning; we need to allow time for it.

We've already talked about reflection, the clasping link in the learning chain. It falls into the category of "worth it in the long run." However, there are walls, tall and thick, to push through at different times during the year. You have to push through their gloom sometimes with nothing more than faith that there is a brighter light on the other side. One of those first walls for me was the initial selection time because I didn't feel the children knew enough and I couldn't teach or model enough to let them internalize valid criteria before that first selection. I was disappointed that so many valued their handwriting. And I felt guilty. Somehow I must have been responsible for those attitudes. Reflection (my own), though, reassured me that their baseline criteria would let me see real growth in their thinking later in the year.

That wall was thick, and it's weight bore heavily for weeks— but the light on the other side was there all the time. The October reflections compared to March and May reflections illuminate growth in every single student! What's more, I now realize that handwriting was important in October because for many students letter formation represented their newest learning. As forming letters became commonplace, handwriting retreated to its proper position—a mere tool.

The children themselves erected the second wall when I announced that it was time for the January selections. "Aww," they groaned, "we'd rather write in our writing folders." How disappointing it was to see them not value their own portfolios. Faith again helped us all through that wall, and perhaps it was the most important one of all. For shortly after that second selection and reflection process, I began to see signs of real internalization and consciousness of their own growth in reading and writing. In our sharing circle, students began to call attention to their strengths, prefacing their comments with, "Did you notice that I told what the book reminded me of?" or "I started to use the word '*ran*' here, but I changed it to '*raced.*' " I also received a note from Mary Beth's mother explaining that Mary Beth had been making her parents aware of her own language growth: "Mama, did you hear me say 'a sea of trees?' That's better than just saying 'a forest.' "

Now let's look at the dimension that's added when students engage in meta-reflection, when they reflect on reflections. Picture the writing portfolio after students have selected and reflected several times. Copies of each selection are stacked in a chronological order in the pocket of a folder. Attached to each selected piece of writing is the written reflection the student made at the time of selection. Most of my students had four such pieces in May when I asked them to read their prior reflections and write a "Dear Reader" letter to introduce their portfolios to other teachers who would be reading them. Jennifer and Daniel wrote the following:

Jennifer

Dear Reader,
    Look on the writer side (of the portfolio) and you will see two copies of books. The two books are called *Jennifer's Family*. My group watches me when I read [these books] to them.
    I have read over 30 books. I published 6 books. I published these two books a long, long time ago.

Daniel

Dear Reader,
    I want you to read *Secrets of the Ninja*. It will be the first book you will see in my portfolio. Look on page 20 for dialect that I didn't know how to do at the beginning of 1st grade.
    I read over 30 books. I've published 8 books. 3 fact books. 5 fiction books. Five plus three is 8.

One additional component of the reflection process I will briefly mention. As part of an ongoing program of parent writing workshops, I invited parents to come to an evening meeting in which part of the agenda would include selecting and writing about a favorite piece from their child's writing folder. Mary Beth's mother brought a piece her child had written at home and added it to the portfolio. I encouraged parents to turn slowly through the pages of their child's work and to comment in every possible positive way. Most wrote a full page letter to their children, glowing over content (I'm glad you included your brother), and style (I like the way you made the monster talk).

Will I continue my portfolio project? Yes, definitely. Portfolios represent the ultimate in learning processes: to know, to know that you know, and to know how you know. Will I conduct it in the same manner? Yes and no. I'll keep the open-ended reflection prompt because I have enjoyed trying to track down the concepts Mary Beth may have picked up from Bonn and those Bonn may have picked up from Kelly, and I have enjoyed seeing the concrete evidence of criteria for good writing my students have internalized. I want to study more carefully the idea that selection criteria might be linked to newly learned competencies as I believe the handwriting was. (What is the relationship between recently learning to write dialogue or metaphor and selecting a piece because it contains dialogue or metaphor?) I'll keep the parental involvement, but I'd like to expand it to include more parents and more selections. I also want to add a procedure in which students will respond to each other's portfolios because I believe it will magnify possibilities for them to learn from each other.

I dream that someone will ask me how I know my students are learning. I have my response prepared: Because THEY know. They talk about learning with each other. They talk with me about their learning, and they reflect on learning when they write about the pieces they choose for their portfolios. Portfolios that are developed over time to include student-selected best works and insights about why each piece is valued by the writer yield a multi-layered, three dimensional view of mental growth. Reflection balances students on Vygotsky's (1978) edge of proximal development, the fine line between what students understand and what they are ready to learn, because it forces the deepest thinking of which they are capable at any given time. Portfolios let us see the best work of the student and his or her personal analysis of competence. Then, adding our own professional eye, we create a clearer picture of each student's growth and learning.

References

Cleary, B. 1960. *Ramona the Brave*. New York: Scholastic.
Dewey, J. 1916. *Democracy and Education*. New York: Macmillan.

Keats, E. J. 1973. *Skates.* New York: Franklin Watts.

Murphy, S., and M. A. Smith. 1991. *Writing Portfolios.* Markham, Ontario: Pippin.

Vygotsky, L. S. 1978. *Mind in Society.* Cambridge, MA: Harvard University Press.

LEARNING GOOD LESSONS: YOUNG READERS RESPOND TO BOOKS

BARBARA BAGGE-RYNERSON
Oyster River Elementary School
Durham, New Hampshire

*O*ne Friday afternoon in early fall, I began to look through the reading journals that my first- and second-grade students were keeping as part of our literature-based reading program. As I looked through the journals I quickly became discouraged by their contents. This lively and entertaining group of children engaged in inspired talk about books throughout the school day. They engaged in meaningful discussions about books, and they responded enthusiastically to the wide range of reading projects that I encouraged them to get involved in. They happily put on puppet shows of favorite books, wrote about the further adventures of The Stupids, and constructed dioramas of favorite storybook scenes.

In sharp contrast, their journal entries were both brief and lifeless. The readers who had written them were nowhere to be found within these brightly constructed, construction paper booklets. I found myself wondering what had gone wrong with their reading journals. I'd read about the use of dialogue journals (Atwell 1987) with older readers. There wasn't much written about using journals with primary students. Perhaps there was a reason for this. Perhaps I was expecting too much from these young readers.

Not wanting to abandon the idea just yet, I decided instead to clarify in my own mind why I thought journals could be valuable for my students and myself. When my students kept science journals, I saw that writing was a way to reflect on their thinking. My hope was that a reading journal would provide them with a way to reflect further on their reading. I had hoped that my students would go beyond factual recall or summarizing. These were not meant to be book reports. I had also hoped that the students would find the journals to be useful reference tools when they were involved in later discussions about their reading. If that was my understanding of the journal, I began to wonder how my students felt about them.

When I returned to school on Monday, I asked the class to tell me what they thought of both their reading journals and their weekly, small-group literature discussions. Their responses made it clear to me that they found their discussion groups both enjoyable and valuable. Alexis explained, "You get to find out what other people thought about the same books that you've read." Katie replied, "I get to find out about good books that I might read. The books that my friends like are usually books that I will like."

When discussing the reading journals, the class was far less enthusiastic. Peter explained that sometimes, "I have nothing to say." I asked them why they thought I required them to keep reading journals. Tyler responded, "So that you and our parents can make sure that we are reading the books." The class' comments made it painfully clear that they saw the discussion groups as an event that they did for their own enjoyment and benefit. Unfortunately, the journal was perceived as being a tool adults used to check up on them.

Their comments made me realize I needed to find ways to show them that their journals could be personally useful. I also had to help them see the journal as a place for their own personal reactions to their reading. They would need me to act as a model and guide in moving them toward this goal.

I decided that my first task would be to encourage my students to use their journals as vehicles for thinking about the personal connections and meanings that they made with books. In order to legitimize and elicit this type of response, I began to keep my own journal, which I regularly shared with the class. Just as the sharing of my own writing had served as a powerful model, these young readers delighted in seeing their teacher as a reader who shared her personal reactions to books.

The first journal entry that I shared with the class was a response that I had written after reading *The Relatives Came* (Rylant, 1985). I read them the lead from this book, which focuses on the relatives packing up their car and getting ready for their trip in the darkness of early morning. I explained to the class that this part of the book always reminds me of the trips that I took as a young child with my family. Then I shared my entry:

> *The Relatives Came* by Cynthia Rylant, has to be one of my all-time favorite books. I don't think I'll ever tire of reading it. It brings back so many childhood memories. When I read the beginning, I'm always reminded of the times when my family would take long car trips together. We would pile into the car so early in the morning that the sky was still dark and the air was still cold. My head always had that mixed up feeling that you get when you are tired and excited at the same time. It always felt like the members of my family all shared a great secret. We were about to embark on an exciting adventure while the rest of the world was still silent and sleeping.

When I shared this and other journal entries in which I talked about the connections that I felt between my own life and the lives of storybook characters, the class slowly began to share the personal connections that they made with books in their own journals. Megan read *The Quilt Story* (Johnston, 1985) and wrote:

> This book is about a quilt that a mother made for her daughter. Her daughter loved it. One day they moved. Her dad built a house and a new rocking horse. She was sad because the only thing that was not new was the quilt. So her mother rocked her and she felt better. I like this book because I have a blanket. But sometimes my sister calls it stupid. It doesn't make me feel good. But the blanket is important to me.

The class seemed more engaged in their journal writing. But they still hit dry spells. There were still times when as Peter put it, "I have nothing to say." Now that I was keeping my own reading journal, I was beginning to run into situations in which I too had nothing to say. Not all writing connects with me in a way that compels me to respond in my journal. If I felt this way as an adult, how overwhelmed these six- and seven-year-olds must be! I must admit that I was also beginning to feel concerned about the amount of time it was taking for some of these children to complete each journal entry. I decided that I needed to legitimize reading for reading's sake. Sometimes you just want to read. I talked it over with the class. We decided that after reading three books and recording the titles in their reading logs, that they would choose their favorite and complete a journal entry in which they would respond to this favorite book. I also gave each child a list of questions that they could refer to when thinking about their reading. They were not restricted to responding to the questions on this list. Instead the list could help children who were occasionally stuck when it was time to complete a journal entry. It read as follows:

Does this story remind you of anything that has ever happened to you?

If you were in the story would you do the same thing that the main character did?

Is there a character that you would like to have as a friend?

Does this book remind you of anything else that you have read?

What do you think the author is trying to tell you?

If you had a chance to talk to the author or illustrator, what would you say or ask?

How did the words or pictures in the book make you feel?

Without the burden of having to write about every book and with the guiding questions, the children began to comment more on the quality of the illustrations and text. They commented on particular aspects of a story they felt were effective. Katie wrote this in her journal after reading *Owl Moon* (Yolen, 1987):

I think the author used beautiful language like when she said, "They walked into a clearing of snow that was whiter than milk in a cereal bowl." I loved the pictures. They matched the words. I have this book at home. It is one of my favorites.

Megan's journal entry also reflects more interest in writing about what she read after reading *Five Secrets in a Box* (Brighton, 1987):

I like the book because of the pictures. When I looked at the title of the book it made me want to know the secrets in the box.

They began to imagine themselves in a character's position. They passed judgment over characters' behaviors. Andy's response to *I Have to Go* (Munsch, 1989) is one example of character examination:

I think it's funny, especially when he has his snowsuit on. . . . The family is concerned that Andrew doesn't have to go pee. I think they're so bogus. They ask Andrew, "Do you have to go pee? Do you have to go pee?" If I was him, I would just go when he has to go.

Dianna also gave her insight into the characters in *Henny Penny* (Zimmerman, 1989):

I like the book Henny Penny. I think that the problem was that Henny Penny and Cocky Locky and Ducky Lucky and Goosey Loosey and Turkey Lurkey followed Foxy Loxy and he ate them. They could of just ignored Foxy Loxy.

They began to compare particular stories to other stories they had read. Sarah's journal entry shows this effort at comparison after reading *Goldilocks and the Three Bears* (Marshall, 1988):

> This reminds me of Red Riding Hood because they both don't listen to their moms.

And David made a comparison after reading *Scaredy Bears* (Young, 1988):

> It's an awesome book. I really think it's like *Goldilocks and the Three Bears* because there were three bears and three bowls of porridge and three chairs.

They often declared a book to be their personal favorite. Megan wrote about her favorite book after reading *Music, Music, for Everyone* (Williams, 1984):

> This is one of my favorite books I have ever read. If I was in the story, I would do the same thing. When I get bigger, I'm going to get to play the flute. I can't wait to do that. My sister is going to play the violin and we will play together.

They also began to comment on the lessons that the authors were trying to teach. After reading *Gorilla* (Browne, 1985) Chris wrote the following analysis:

> It is about a girl who liked a gorilla. The gorilla came to life and brought her to the zoo. The author is trying to tell parents to spend more time with their children.

Tyler's journal entry, which has a drawing as well as text (see Figure 1), makes this insightful point about *Bill and Pete* (de Paola, 1978):

> The man shouldn't of started to capture crocodiles. Bill was good to teach the man a lesson. If Pete wasn't his toothbrush, he would be a suitcase now.

Asking for fewer entries, continually serving as a model for my students and helping them to see the wide range of response possibilities, these were ways in which I helped my students respond to books more easily. But I also had to change the type of feedback that I was writing in their journals. While looking through their earlier entries, I realized that I had responded to their brief, underdeveloped comments by interrogating these readers. My responses to their entries looked like the types of

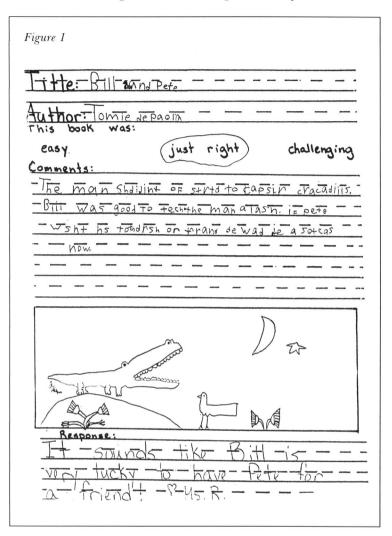

Figure 1

questions one might find in the teacher's guide to a basal reader. David's entry was typical of the way in which I barraged the reader with questions.

Here is David's response to *Mrs. Beggs and the Wizard* (Mayer, 1973):

If I was Mrs. Beggs I wouldn't care about the wizard.

Here is my response to his journal entry:

Did she care about the wizard? How do you know? Why shouldn't she care about him?

At least David answered my questions (though *very* briefly). Sarah was decidedly less cooperative. Sarah's response to *A Lost Button* from *Frog and Toad are Friends* (Lobel, 1970) was

> Frog gets a jacket. At the end it was funny.

My response to her entry was

> Why did he get a jacket?

Sarah wrote back

> I do not know.

Sarah certainly made it clear that I had better change my approach if I expected her to engage in any form of dialogue with me. Obviously my role needed to change. Instead of interrogating these readers, my responses needed to tell the children that what they had to say was valid and important. Instead of asking questions, I began to share my own reactions to a story. If a child seemed to enjoy a book, I would recommend another book in the same genre or another title written by the same author. I would let them know when their insights surprised me or changed my thinking about the story. Sometimes my comments merely let them know that I had read their entry and that their comments encouraged me to either read the book again or to read it for the first time. I now rarely ask the children questions in their journals. If I do ask a question, it is because I am curious about their opinions, not because I am testing their comprehension. In other words, I don't ask questions that I know the answer to. I also explained to them that they are more than welcome to talk with me about the question during our next conference rather than writing me a reply. I was surprised to find that when I stopped asking questions, the students sometimes wrote back to me anyway.

Sarah's response (Figure 2) after reading *Miss Nelson Is Missing* (Allard and Marshall, 1978) was as follows:

> I would do the same thing that Miss Nelson did if I were a teacher and my kids were bad.

I wrote back to Sarah:

> It certainly did seem to work. Sometimes people need to be reminded that they really are lucky.

Sarah wrote back to me:

> Dear Mrs. Rynerson,
>
> I am so glad that the kids learned their lesson. I do that [play a trick] to my brother when he does not shut up because I am trying to concentrate on a book.
>
> From,
Sarah P

Instead of always trying to engage in dialogue through reading journals, I decided to build in time to talk with a child about his or her journal during reading conferences. I began to ask children to share their journal entries as a springboard for our conversations about books. This I hoped would help them to see their journals not as a way for me to check up on them but, instead, as a way for them to share their thinking with me.

I also began to encourage the class to share their journals with one another during peer reading conferences and literature discussion groups. This way the journals would serve as a tool for recording their thoughts to share later on with their peers. The journals would, I hoped, be of personal use to the students rather than just a requirement from me.

Over the course of the school year, I saw that my students became more comfortable with the task of responding in their journals. Their journals were also beginning to take on a more meaningful role during literature discussions, peer reading conferences, and reading conferences with teachers. Most importantly the children took pleasure in making connections between the lives of storybook characters and their own experiences. In the process they drew their own meanings from the text.

In the spring Lauren wrote the following entry after reading *Goldilocks and the Three Bears* (Marshall, 1988):

> This book reminds me of when my mother said not to sneak cookies and I did. But I learned a good lesson because there was a spider in the jar and it scared me half to death.

By watching and listening to these young readers I also learned a good lesson.

References:

Allard, Harry and James Marshall. 1974. *The Stupids Step Out.* Boston: Houghton Mifflin.

Figure 2

Title: Miss nelson is Missing

Author: James MarShalt

This book was:

easy.   (just right)   challenging

Comments:

I wode Do the Sarre thing that MiSS Netsou Did if I were a tec.her and My kids were → Bad

Response:

It certainly soound to work Sometimes pepiro need to be remirdes that they realy are lucky

Dear Ms. Rynerson,

I am so glat that the kids lert thar lasin. I do that to my bather wane he has not shut up becase I am trting to cosintrat on a book

From,
Sarah P.

————. 1977. *Miss Nelson is Missing.* Boston: Houghton Mifflin.

————. 1978a. *The Stupids Die.* Boston: Houghton Mifflin.

————. 1978b. *The Stupids Have a Ball.* Boston: Houghton Mifflin.

Atwell, Nancie. 1987. *In the Middle.* Portsmouth, NH: Heinemann.

Browne, Anthony. 1985. *Gorilla.* New York: Alfred A. Knopf.

Brighton, Catherine. 1987. *Five Secrets in a Box.* New York: E. P. Dutton.

de Paola, Tomie. 1978. *Bill and Pete.* New York: G.P. Putnam's.

Johnston, Tony. 1985. *The Quilt Story.* New York: Scholastic.

Lobel, Arnold. 1970. *Frog and Toad Are Friends.* New York: Harper & Row.

Marshall, James. 1988. *Goldilocks and the Three Bears.* New York: Scholastic.

Mayer, Mercer. 1973. *Mrs. Beggs and the Wizard.* New York: Parents' Magazine.

Munsch, Robert. 1989. *I Have to Go!* Toronto, Canada: Annick.

Rylant, Cynthia. 1985. *The Relatives Came.* New York: Bradbury.

Williams, Vera B. 1984. *Music, Music for Everyone.* New York: The Trumpet Club.

Yolen, Jane. 1987. *Owl Moon.* New York: Philomel.

Young, Christine. 1988. *Scaredy Bears.* Bothell, WA: The Wright Group.

Zimmerman, H. Werner. 1989. *Henny Penny.* New York: Scholastic.

KRISTIN'S STORY:
A MORAL VOICE EMERGES

MAUREEN BARBIERI
Laurel School
Shaker Heights, Ohio

*T*he knowledge about relationships and the life of relationships that flourish on this remote island of female adolescence are. . . . like notes from the underground.

Carol Gilligan

They gather in clusters before and between classes, these child-women, twelve and thirteen years old. They hold whispered conversations behind locker doors, huddled around window benches: "He said what?" "Do you think he's going to call her?" "How do you know he didn't mean it?" "Are you sure?" They plan elaborate meetings for later: "You call me." "My mom said she can drive if we can get a ride home." "I can only have two people sleep over. Call me." "Chris said Joe might call to-night. . . ."

The clusters shift. Who is in this week? Who the victim of cruel taunting: "Do you suppose you'll always be flat-chested?"

Seventh-grade life at an all girls' school. Psychologist Carol Gilligan et al (1990) writes of the innate female need for relation-ship, for connectedness. The need by the time girls reach seventh grade is so strong, she says, that many "go underground" with their honest opinions, ideas, and questions. Rather than risk the disapproval of the group, girls will make compromises, saying or doing things they don't really believe in, to ensure their contin-ued inclusion.

"We know it's wrong to pick on someone," Laurel seventh graders often say, "but it's worth it, if it gets you in with the popular kids."

Protesting small cruelties becomes all but impossible for girls like Kristin. They fear being ostracized; their not condoning the nasty remarks may ultimately lead to their being the next victims. And their strongest desire is to belong. Such a pressing need to connect, according to Gilligan, is both normal and necessary. Girls must, however, come to terms with the other developmental task facing them at this time—the need to assert their independence, their individuality.

The more I read Gilligan's research, the more sensitive I became to what was going on in the seventh grade. How could I, as their English teacher, help them deal with such weighty issues? Writing had been at the heart of my curriculum for more than eight years, and I had seen its power and its magic at work in classrooms long before I found myself at Laurel School. But for girls, writing is even more crucial than I had believed, for it is often through writing that girls are able to break through their silences and discover what they really think and feel.

Kristin's need became clear when we embarked on our study of fiction. In lieu of total free choice in reading and writing, I had decided to examine with the girls a specific genre each trimester. I had reconsidered my long-held belief that students need constant and absolute choice in both reading and writing. Instead of preventing them from writing with authority and commitment, the genre structure enabled them to become engaged with their writing in more compelling ways, giving them new lenses on their worlds, on themselves.

I had never felt particularly comfortable teaching or writing fiction, and from time to time I had wondered whether it was even necessary in the busy school year. My girls wrote memoir, persuasion, poetry, even essays, well, but their fiction, like my own, felt pretty flat. But as I thought more and more about the power of literature in our lives, I became intrigued with the notion of really learning to write fiction with my students.

Jack Wilde (Hansen, Newkirk, and Graves, 1985) suggests that students concentrate on plausibility and a change in a character. We used these parameters when we began our fiction writing at Laurel. But before our characters could change, we realized, we had to know who they were in the first place.

We followed Donald Graves' recommendation that we assume the persona of the character and let classmates conduct interviews in turn (Graves, 1989). Each student became her character, and through the interview process, discovered minute details of that person's life, past and present. Flesh and blood characters emerged on the page, as we spent days in writing workshops making notes, doing free writing, and sketching maps of their lives. "I love these exercises," Kristin said. "Can we do more of this?" After about a week of prewriting, some were eager to begin plotting their stories.

Kristin was itching to write. I listened in conference, as the piece grew, nudging her by asking questions when I felt genuinely curious: "Who was Molly?" "What was her part in the story?" "Why was this such a difficult decision for Cathy to make?" Kristin was soon bursting with pride as she read the piece to the class.

No matter how long I work with young people, they continue to perplex, astonish, and delight me; but this was something new. Kristin had discovered, in her writing, a way to examine her own existential dilemma.

Her story, "Friends Mean All the World," is about a group of girls, a bit younger than Kristin and her friends. Cathy, the main character, observes the popular kids taunting shy, awkward, lonely Anne. Molly, Cathy's friend, participates in this behavior and exhibits contempt for Anne.

> "Hey ugly, by the wall!" It was Dan, the school bully. All faces turned to see who it was, and laughter filled the air. I stood there with my mouth open.
> "How could they be so mean?" I asked myself.
> I felt for Anne, who was now kicking a rock back and forth. Soon the bell rang, signaling that it was time to go in. Molly and Beth came running up to me with broad smiles on their faces. Molly looked as though she was going to explode with the new gossip she had. I wanted to mention to her what had happened to Anne, but I didn't know how to say it.

"I didn't know how to say it" seems a predominant and nagging state of mind for Cathy, as it is for Kristin. It became clear to me that she was writing about herself. This was a story, not only of Cathy, Molly, and Anne but also—and more importantly—of Kristin, Emily, Naeta, Erica, Brady, and the other girls in this seventh-grade class.

> "Listen!" Molly grabbed my arm. "Don't feel bad for her. You're just wasting your time."
> "Ya, O.K.," I agreed reluctantly.

> That day walking home for me was different. I felt strange. What had happened to Anne that day seemed to have had an effect on me. I tried pushing out the guilty feeling. But why did I feel guilty? I had never done anything to her, or had I? Maybe all the times she was made fun of I should have protected her or at least said something in her favor. But what would the crowd say? It would be awful if they thought I liked her, and they'd start making fun of me and hating me.

Gilligan (1982) terms Cathy's response an exercise of the voice of care. Cathy cannot push Anne's pain from her mind because she knows that, in some way, she is connected to Anne.

But Cathy is also concerned with other connections. She needs to sustain her membership in, her connection to, the group that tolerates, indeed encourages, the cruel behavior. It is Kristin's struggle every day.

Following Wilde's admonition that fiction be plausible, Kristin did not allow her character to change too rapidly.

> I felt as though maybe, if I forgot about what had happened at school and didn't dwell on it, I wouldn't feel bad anymore. . . . The next day in school, I reminded myself not to say anything to any of my friends about Anne. I really didn't want them to think I felt sorry for her; then they would think I was like Anne. . . . I started picking the players when I saw Anne in her usual place by the wall. Something inside me told me to ask her to play, but I dared not for fear of embarrassment.

Cathy's compassion for Anne is now in direct conflict with her desire to please her friends. She knows what is right, but she questions whether doing the right thing will be worth the price she will pay. When Cathy articulates her concern for Anne, she is met with scorn:

> "Oh, and now you're protecting her? What is wrong with you?"

Sure enough, Cathy's friends begin to exclude her from their games at recess, confirming her worst fears.

> I felt awful. Embarrassment and anger filled my body. I could feel my face getting red as a beet. I wanted to run inside and cry. Millions of thoughts started going through my mind. Why is the crowd turning on me? I didn't do anything to them. Just because I was nice to Anne, they were ignoring me. But then it hit me. Why was I nice to Anne? Who cared about her? She probably didn't even care that I had called her. Why did I sacrifice all my friends for a squeaky-voiced kid who didn't even care about friends?"

Here Cathy feels a strong pull back to the familiar world of friends. Why trade the known for the unknown? It was a dilemma I knew Kristin faced often. There were girls in our class like Anne, isolated, shy, left out of things.

> Slowly my thoughts changed as I saw Anne by the wall. She was a sad kid who maybe didn't know how to get friends. . . . Maybe friends take time to come, and Anne didn't know how to get friends.
> I really felt sorry for Anne right at that moment. All this time people were mean to her, and she never had anyone to be with, and my being mean to her only added to her misery.
> That day I think many ridges formed in my brain, because I learned a lot. Just that little incident at recess made me realize a very valuable lesson. There is nothing better than a true and honest friendship, and a good friend means all the world. . . . It would be hard to become friends with Anne. I would have to accept a lot of name-calling and teasing. But I felt if Anne could handle it, so could I. . . . I felt good, good enough to invite Anne over to my house.

Cathy had resolved her dilemma. Her care voice and her justice voice (Gilligan, 1982) came together in harmony, her need to assert herself and her need to maintain her connection to others reconciled to some degree. But what of Kristin? And what of me? What had we learned here?

Kristin had learned to write a piece of fiction that examined a real issue. She had written what she'd needed to write.

"We write to think," says Murray (1985), "to be surprised by what appears on the page; to explore our world with language; to discover meaning that teaches us and that may be worth sharing with others."

Kristin had used her writing to think. Was she aware of what she had done? At the end of each trimester each student presents her portfolio, first to me in conference and then to her parents at home. In her letter to her parents, reflecting on her growth in English that trimester, Kristin wrote:

> This trimester I have really learned a lot in writing fiction. Fiction is harder than nonfiction because you have to come up with stories that never happened to you. I know that sometimes it is easier to get your fiction ideas from real things that have happened in your life. You have to make sure that you don't start writing the real story.
> I had a lot of trouble coming up with my idea. I finally got my idea from thinking about my old school and how I always felt sorry for a girl named Beth. I didn't at all have the same amount of courage that "Cathy" my main character does. . . .

Kristin found her story idea in her past experience. However, I would also maintain, she did more. In allowing Cathy to demonstrate courage, Kristin tries on a new behavior, resisting peer pressure. She uses her writing to live, not merely in retrospect but in projection. In this story Kristin charts what may well be her own future development.

In thinking about Gilligan's work, I knew that Kristin's story had implications for all my students. This story needed to be shared beyond the usual oral readings and publication in the school magazine. With Kristin's eager permission, I photocopied the piece and asked the whole class to read it and respond in writing in their notebooks, the same way they did with other literature they read.

"This sounds a lot like our class. I think it's interesting how Cathy thinks Molly is practically her best friend," writes Wallis, ever the pragmatist, exercising her own justice voice. "If Cathy felt so apprehensive about telling Colleen her opinion, I wouldn't consider her my best friend."

Brady seems to appreciate the complexities of Cathy's situation and sees, more than most girls, what the character's actions cost her:

> I thought this story was very good and it expressed a very important topic which, I think a lot of people in our class can relate to. I don't think anyone completely understands how hard it is to put yourself in the position that Cathy put herself in. Although it is hard for Anne, she is used to all of the name calling and has lived with it up until now. Cathy isn't used to not having any friends, and at first Cathy doesn't want to lose all of her friends. By the end she finally realizes that if her friends won't like her because of Anne, they're not her true friends. This is a big step and obviously this shows a lot of maturity and confidence in Cathy.

Caroline writes:

> In this story, I really liked how Cathy acted. At times, I've wondered what it would be like to do that myself. Would I lose all my friends? Or would they just get closer? The title is true though, and I feel thankful for all my friends. I think that probably if this did happen, they would get farther away from me. I guess for this reason, I've never seriously thought about doing this. This story really got its point across. It really left me thinking.

Discussing the story in class, beyond its strengths as a piece of writing, was hard for these girls. After all, the issues were close to home. They wrote with candor and insight, and I knew the story had, as Caroline put it, left them thinking. In taking an honest look at herself in the story, Kristin helped her classmates do the same thing. Her writing made a difference, not only to her but to all of us.

Kristin's mother says it best. She appreciated what had gone on and wrote a response for Kristin to save in her portfolio, articulating what fiction writing had done for her daughter:

> We loved your story about Cathy and Anne and respected your absolute honesty when you said you weren't as brave as Cathy. How true, Kristin! It's difficult to take a stand and be alone with only your principles. Yet, you know you are growing into a person like Cathy because you are able to recognize that she has integrity. Good for you.

References

Gilligan, Carol. 1982. *In a Different Voice: Psychological Theory and Women's Development.* Cambridge, MA: Harvard University Press.

Gilligan, Carol, Nona P. Lyons, and Trudy J. Hanmer, eds. 1990. *Making Connections: The Relational Worlds of Adolescent Girls at Emma Willard School.* Cambridge, MA: Harvard University Press.

Gilligan, Carol, Janie Victoria Ward, and Jill McLean Taylor, eds. with Betty Bardige. 1988. *Mapping the Moral Domain.* Cambridge, MA: Harvard University Press.

Graves, Donald. 1989. *Experiment with Fiction.* Portsmouth, NH: Heinemann.

Hansen, Jane, Thomas Newkirk, and Donald Graves, eds. 1985. *Breaking Ground: Teachers Relate Reading and Writing in the Elementary School.* Portsmouth, NH: Heinemann.

Murray, Donald M. 1985. *A Writer Teaches Writing.* Boston: Houghton Mifflin.

WRITING
AND THE ARTS

"ANY COMMENTS OR QUESTIONS?" RECOGNIZING A GOOD STORY PLAY AND WRITING ONE

MONA HALABY
Mills College Children's School
Oakland, California

*I*n my classroom, a first-second-third-grade combination, some children are painting backdrops, some are putting costumes together, others are writing invitations, while still others are rehearsing their parts on stage. We are getting ready for our annual spring production of story plays to be performed for parents and friends.

I first became acquainted with story plays three years ago when reading Vivian Paley's (1981) *Wally's Stories.* In Paley's preschool classroom students dictate their own stories to a teacher, and then act them out at circle time. I became convinced that dictated stories could play a unique role in young children's language/writing development. So I decided to give my students a daily opportunity to dictate story plays and act them out at circle.

"Mona, may I sign up on the waiting list to dictate a story play?" Lakeisha asks. She and Elizabeth have been deliberating about their joint play. I tell Lakeisha to finish her reading first, and that I'll call her when Brendan is done dictating his story play. Brendan is sitting by my side, deep in thought. His play is entitled *The Rocket*:

> Once upon a time there was a fish that swimmed in his own blood. Then King Tut came to give him his food, and it was made out of skeleton bones and blood and bodies.

111

Brendan is exploring the themes of the Halloween season. He is attempting to master his own fears. Later in the day when the children sit at the circle, Brendan stands in the middle, and asks for volunteers to act in his play, "I'm going to be the fish," he declares, "Who wants to be King Tut?" Many hands shoot up in feverish supplication. Brendan chooses Andrew. No one is surprised. These two have been inseparable lately. The rest of the class sits back. I hear grumblings. "It's not fair! He always picks his buddies!" We've discussed this issue before. As a class we've come to the conclusion that the author has certain privileges, and picking one's actors is one of them.

We are ready to start now. The room is silent. Brendan and the actors he has selected rest against the chalkboard, waiting for their cue to appear in the center of the circle, our stage. I start reading: "*The Rocket*, a play by Brendan. Once upon a time there was a fish that swimmed in his own blood. . . ." Brendan lunges on his tummy into the circle, motioning rapid breast strokes. Some children in the audience giggle at his unabashed enthusiasm; some show unease or disgust at the word "blood," while others look transported to a different time and place. At the end of the play when I read, "The End," the magic spell is broken. In an instant we are back to the reality of our classroom. The audience claps and cheers. The actors return to the circle, except for Brendan, who then sits in the author's chair to solicit comments or questions from his audience. "Brendan, how can you swim in your own blood?" they ask. Brendan is not quite sure himself. He tries to explain the gory images from his play. He has aroused their curiosity.

I am ready for Lakeisha now. She and Elizabeth sit on either side of me at the writing table. "Our play is called *Teenage Mutant Ninja Girls*," Elizabeth smiles. I write down their title and the date. They start, each one dictating a piece, as though it springs from a shared unconscious:

> Once upon a time there was Teenage Mutant Ninja girls: Kelly Turtle, Emily Turtle, Morgan Turtle, Ellen Turtle, and Lara Kitty who was their pet, plus there was their master Princess. The Teenage Mutant girls fought the bad witch, and the witch had two helpers, one was a bad Baby Ruff Ruff, and the other was a mean mutt. They sat home and they ate pizza and ice cream. . . . The next morning the Teenage Mutant Ninja girls saw the witch. The witch said, "Teenage Mutant Ninja girls, I'll get you, and my baby Ruff Ruff will get you, too." "No, you won't." They ran home, and asked their master if she had any plans to catch the witch. She said, "I have a plan." And the

plan was to get some water and pour it on the witch, but the plan didn't work.

The girls continue to dictate. Their play is filled with elaborate schemes, aborted plans, rescue missions, animated dialogues, and by the end, the Ninja girls kill the witch and live happily ever after. When the girls act out their play at circle time, the boys are slightly offended at first, almost as though some sacrilegious act has taken place. "Teenage Mutant Ninja Turtles are supposed to be boys," I hear them mutter, but as the play progresses, the boys see its irony and humor. And at the end the girls receive numerous compliments for their creativity. One boy, though, asks, "How come you didn't have any boys in your play?" Lakeisha grins and says nonchalantly, "We just didn't feel like it."

Morgan and Emily's story play *The Native Habitat* does not have a happy ending:

> One day a little girl was walking in the forest. She found a baby bunny, and she took it home. But there was a hunter in the forest. But the little girl didn't know. And she asked the bunny to go pick berries. Then she heard bullets. The little girl ran outside, and the bunny was laying there. The little girl called the doctor. The doctor tried to teach the bunny how to talk. Suddenly the bunny said, "Death! Death!" The doctor called the little girl and said to the girl, "The bunny is dead." The End.

After the children perform the play at circle time, someone asks the authors, "Why did you write a sad play?" Morgan answers, "Well, it's okay to have sad plays too, you know. These things can happen." Some children are incensed at what they interpret as the little girl's negligence; others are furious at the hunter for shooting the bunny, others at the doctor's inability to save the bunny. But all in all the children reluctantly accept this slice of reality amidst their circle. After Morgan and Emily's story play the other students feel encouraged to explore more diverse endings. It is as though *The Native Habitat* gives everyone the permission to write plays with sad endings.

Story plays allow Eliot, who has dyslexia, to participate in our literary activities. Eliot's dictation starts with the narrator presenting the background to *Mystery Aboard the NNX 12*:

> The NNX 12 is an imperial planetary war ship. It is only used for imperial fighting, but can be sent out on missions requiring the

strongest and fastest vessels in the galaxy. . . . The crew is ready to board the vessel. If their mission is discovered, these men may easily die. But their luck will hold, because the Captain is a wise and experienced man.

We discuss the merits of introducing one's characters and background at the beginning of the play, and it becomes apparent to the class that this particular structure gives the audience a lot of facts. From Eliot's prologue we know that the NNX 12 is strong and fast, that the Captain is wise and experienced, and that this mission is dangerous. And Eliot's rich and dramatic dialogue keeps us on the edge of our seats:

CAPTAIN ELIOT: Where in the world did I put that darn lap top computer? It's a secret computer. My plans were in there for the NNX 12. Radio Technician Andrew, have you seen it?
RADIO TECHNICIAN ANDREW: No, sir. Maybe you should ask Astronomer Michael.

From the moment I introduced story plays to my class, I recognized the success of this learning tool. The children were immediately engaged. They were literally lining up to dictate their stories, and when it came to acting them out, almost everyone's hand was raised in the hopes of being selected by the author for a part in the play. I tend to rely on my intuition when I see how enthusiastically children respond to an activity. But because I believe that teaching is also an intellectual process, I wanted to look beyond the children's enthusiasm to the possible literary merits inherent in this language experience. Here are additional merits I've observed:

- Freed from the mechanics of the written language, young writers can dictate stories far more complex than they can realistically write themselves at this age. Moreover, the speed with which a teacher can take down a story dictation far exceeds the laborious writing of most six- and seven-year-olds.
- As the children sit by my side and I write down their stories, I am modeling appropriate writing conventions, such as directionality of print, capitalization, spelling, paragraphing, punctuation, and more. I try to respect their choice of words and themes.
- By dictating stories, children join the long oral tradition of storytellers who weave their tales not only with words but also with voice intonations and inflections, facial expressions and hand gestures. Their stories come alive.

- Because I believe that we need to allow and promote authentic contexts for learning in our classrooms, reading and writing need to be meaningful and make sense to the children. Story plays are meaningful because they reflect the children's interests and concerns, from princesses and fairies to Ninja Turtles and superheroes. The forces of evil and the forces of good interact each day at our circle.
- Story plays give young children who cannot revise their writing yet an opportunity to edit what they see dramatized. Story plays provide a visual and kinesthetic experience.
- The children are learning about each other, too. Their classmates, for example, keep exploring the same themes: Michelle's repeated stories about princesses and puppies captured by wicked witches, Andrew's military plots, Lara's story plays about cats and dogs getting lost. They also know that Emily plays a good fairy, light on her feet, that Michelle makes a great puppy who can bark and yelp, that Eliot plays the part of the villain with relish.
- Not only do story plays help improve writing skills but they also help children *decenter* (a Piagetian term referring to the cognitive growth inherent in becoming aware of someone else's point of view). When someone in the audience asks, "But I don't get it! How did the princess escape if she was trapped in the dungeon?" At this point the author is confronted with someone else's perspective. Subsequently, the thinking process, coupled with the social exchange that follows, can provoke much cognitive growth. Invariably, the author returns to his or her play to revise the text, and by taking the audience's response into consideration, makes it more coherent.
- While I read the dictated stories at circle time, the actors pantomime the actions described. When there's a dialogue, they repeat their lines after me. Being actors requires that the children be attentive. It provides them with an opportunity to listen, interpret, and enact. If I read that the Ninja Turtles are eating pizza, then the actors pretend to eat. If instead of eating they pretend to fight, I remind them to respect the author's words.
- Last, but not least, story plays provide the children with the magic of seeing their words come alive on stage. Their characters move and talk, stirring the audience with sentiment, laughter, and tears.

This year before we selected the plays to be performed at our spring production, I decided to read to the children myths and fairy tales from around the world. Each day we read stories ranging from old favorites, such as *Rumpelstiltskin* and *Cinderella*, to more obscure ones, such as *The Magic Wings* (China) and *The Prince Who Knew His Fate* (Ancient Egypt). My goal was twofold: on the one hand, I wanted to expose the children to more culturally diverse fiction, and on the other, I wanted them to develop a critical literary sense.

First, I wanted them to become aware that not all fairy tales take place in a wooded forest with the wicked witch, the beautiful princess, the handsome prince. Not all good stories end with "and they lived happily ever after." Not all female characters are rescued by male heroes. I am especially interested in balancing the more stereotypical female roles (and incidentally male roles, too) with more creative, nonstereotypical roles. It is important for young children to have a multitude of role models, to have choices, and to make their own decisions when they grow up.

Second, I wanted my students to develop a discerning eye for what constitutes a good story. Each day after listening to a story, the children gave their opinions, and so we started a list that we kept posted near the circle. The title of the list was "What Makes For a Good Story?" After just one week the children came up with a comprehensive list:

plot
setting
heroes and villains
mystery
magic
imagination
details
good beginning and end
something happy or sad
surprises
loss of something important
weddings! (Ah! What can I say? I'm trying! It's not easy to break down these deeply rooted childhood fantasies!)

By trusting my students, I had invited surprises into my classroom. Not unlike high school and college students who grapple with English literature courses, my students, too, were recognizing what constitutes good literary content. They were becoming reflective, sophisticated readers.

My immediate goal, though, was to inspire the children to write or dictate story plays that would be rich with some of the features from the list we'd developed in class. All of this in time for our production! And Kelly did—Kelly, a strong, prolific writer, six years of age. Her story was about a mean little girl who rather magically becomes kind and sweet. It was a beautiful transformation story—the archetypal story of human redemption, of hope, of second chances, of gained wisdom and experience. I was charmed by Kelly's piece. However, it did not contain many details. Would it grab the attention of our audience? I wanted to include it in our production, but it needed some fleshing out. Yet, how could I do a mini-lesson on editing with six- and seven-year-olds? What about their autonomy? Won't it be too directive? Our daily story plays never get edited. Would Kelly still retain ownership of her play? Would this process of editing inhibit my writers in the future?

I decide to talk to Kelly alone first. I tell her she has a good story, but she needs to add more details. Does she want to work on it at home, at writers' workshop, or with the class at circle time? Kelly quickly jumps at the opportunity to share her work with her classmates. So the next day she reads her story play to the class. Her opening line reads, "Once there was a girl and she was mean." I ask the class, "What do you know from Kelly's first line?" Someone volunteers, "We know that it's a girl and that she's mean." That's a beginning. Then someone adds, "We need to know more about her." Perfect, I think. "What else would you like to know about this girl?" I ask. Lots of hands go up. "What's her name?" "How old is she?" "What does she look like?" "Where does she live?" The children are completely engaged. Kelly looks thrilled. I ask her, "Kelly, do you have an idea for a name for your character, or would you like some suggestions from the class?" She wants suggestions. Hands go up again. Someone says, "Christina." Kelly likes that name. Christina will be eight. That is decided by Kelly. Then other children share their thoughts about Christina's looks. Kelly receives their suggestions, accepting some, rejecting others. The process of creation feels inclusive of the whole class, yet Kelly still remains in charge. "Where does Christina live?" Someone suggests New York; someone Chicago, Hawaii. Kelly isn't convinced. Then Michael says, "You can make up your own name of a place, like Dr. Seuss does in his stories." Wonderful, I think. Michael is inviting Dr. Seuss to our circle. We are in the company of writers, working at our craft, relying on good models in literature to invent one moment, borrow the next, create, adapt. Kelly likes Michael's idea. She calls her place "The Land of Girls and Boys." Finally, I ask, "What is Christina like when she's mean?" Kelly knows exactly what constitutes meanness. For this young author being mean consists of grabbing things from other people's hands, yelling in people's ears, pulling puppies' ears and tails, and talking with your mouth full! Now we have a story play rich and bursting with details. Here are excerpts from Kelly's revised version:

> Once upon a time in the Land of Girls and Boys, there was a little girl named Christina, and she was very, very mean. Christina was eight years old. She had brown curly, long hair, and she wore a blue bow on the top of her head.

> Christina did lots of bad things, like she screamed in her mother's ear while her mother was talking on the phone, and she ate with her mouth open, and she had very bad manners, and when she pet dogs, she pulled their ears and pulled their puppy tails. And at school she played tricks on her teacher, and she grabbed things away from other kids, even if the other kids weren't done. Christina was very, very mean.

At the end of the day I marvel at my students' level of inquiry, their willingness to grow, to think, to immerse themselves in exploring the writing process.

Good teaching means taking risks. Good teaching means revising what I do in light of my own discoveries. Good teaching means demonstrating what it involves to be immersed in literacy; it means inviting my students to share their worlds with one another. Good teaching means always expecting high standards and excellence from my students and from myself.

It is, finally, the day when all those pages of writing, all the thinking, the revising, the talking, all those words and feelings are going to come to life in front of a larger audience. I sit by the side of the stage, and read out loud page after page while my students act out their parts. There is quiet and reverence in the audience, pleasure, and awe while parents and friends sit mesmerized by the plays. It's as though we all understand the power and magic of language.

Then, at the end, as I stand on the sidelines of the stage, tears in my eyes, moved by my students' growth, by their joyful, uninhibited celebration of life, Kelly marches on stage in front of her audience, and asks with confidence and glee, "Do you have any comments or questions?"

References

Manniche, Lise. 1981. *The Prince Who Knew His Fate*. New York: Philomel Books.

Paley, Vivian. 1981. *Wally's Stories*. Cambridge, MA: Harvard University Press.

Perrault, Charles. 1988. *Cinderella*. New York: Knopf.

Wolkstein, Diane. 1983. *The Magic Wings*. New York: Dutton.

Zelinsky, Paul. 1986. *Rumpelstiltskin*. New York: Dutton.

STRENGTHENING CHILDREN'S LITERARY VOICES: OPERA IN THE CLASSROOM

SHARON BLECHER
KATHY JAFFEE
Eastwood School
Oberlin, Ohio

*G*iving learners a choice in the form in which they are to represent their understandings (*e.g.*, in literature) in effect gives them a choice that reflects their own conceptualization of the world.

Eliot Eisner

Tonia and Ariel bound into the classroom. They have a definite purpose in mind. Both girls grab a special book from the shelf and sit down to read together. Their heads are touching as they work through the difficult text. One is a much stronger reader than the other, but together they are making sense of the material. This is the third day in a row that the girls have been reading *Aida*, retold by Leontyne Price. When class meeting starts, they don't even look up. These girls, along with forty-two other first and second graders, have just spent a year completely immersed in opera, and they can't get enough of it.

When we started the Opera Project, initiated by Cleveland Opera with the help of Opera America, we did not realize how far-reaching the effects would be. We never saw the sort of resistance to opera that is sometimes seen in adults. It may have been because our first and second graders were already familiar with the idea of telling stories through song. In the past, we had developed classroom operas to retell fairy tales. The children fit their words to a melody like *Skip to My Lou*:

Skip, skip, skip to my Lou
Skip, skip, skip to my Lou
Skip, skip, skip to my Lou
Skip to my Lou, my darling.

In the hands of our first and second graders this became

I am the first little pig
I am the first little pig
I am the first little pig
I am building a house of sticks

There was no writing down of lines and no memorization involved. They could change words here and there as long as the words made sense in the story. Telling stories using the medium of opera seemed like a natural extension of what we had already been doing. Or the lack of resistance may have been due to the fact that the children had no preconceived notions of opera. We were expecting our students to respond to the music, even with the words sung in the original German, and they did. But how did a heterogeneous group of six- and seven-year-olds become so excited about a topic that many adults find intimidating? How did opera become something with which they felt so comfortable?

During November and December, as the children entered the room we played the overture to *The Magic Flute*. They had opportunities to watch videotapes and to read, write, and tell versions of the story. This immersion in *The Magic Flute* helped students with and without experience in the arts begin to develop a common language. Carrie, who was still a beginning reader in November, hadn't yet made the leap that letters and sounds make words. But when we met in a circle to retell *The Magic Flute*, she showed she had a real sense of story. She remembered the smallest details that the rest of the class had forgotten. She knew that the Wild Beasts showed up when Tamino played the flute. She knew that Tamino fell in love with Pamina after looking at her picture. The energy coming through in her voice was infectious. She helped get the rest of the class excited about recalling details of the story.

Tim, a student with a learning disability who usually came late to school, suddenly started appearing on time. As he walked in the door, he would ask if we were going to see more of *The Magic Flute* tape. Domonique negotiated with her Chapter I reading teacher to avoid leaving the room during our *Magic Flute* time. Micah, in his excitement about the opera study, made a flute out of aluminum foil and paper towel tubes. Not content to wait until the class found out the ending to *The Magic Flute*, Tonia borrowed the tape from our public library and watched it several times at home.

Michael became so involved with *The Magic Flute* that he wrote a story about meeting and eventually living with the birdman Papageno.

> I was walking along and wisling. And I hard a wisle. And I soe a man with birds. And his name was Papageno. And he said, I am Papageno. I am a good gie. I said my name is Michael. Papageno said, can we be friends? I said, that is ok with me. But one day Papageno had to leve. Becase he had to go to mery Papagena. And I had to say goodby. Years past by. But one day he came back. He said that his wife dide. Noe we can live togethr I said. And we lived happly ever after."

Michael understood Papageno. He knew him so well that Papageno had become a friend. Michael also knew that in the opera, Papageno had to marry Papagena. But this didn't stop him from continuing the story in a way that allowed him to keep the birdman with him all the time. Papagena died so that Papageno could live happily ever after with Michael!

Sarah, a fluent reader and successful writer, wanted the Princess Pamina to be a friend. She used writing as a way of bringing the character closer. This was her draft:

> I was in the class alone. Actually with my friend, Annie. We were watching The Magic Flute. Then sodenley the screen went blank. There stood Princess Pamina. She said, "I've lost Tamino forever. We said, "No, you haven't. He's just in the Test of Silence. He still loves you. "That's very good," Pamina said. Annie asked her if she wanted a tour of our classroom. Pamina said that would be terrific. We went rite to work. There's one more place, I said, the reading area. And there was Tamino standing. He kneeled. Pamina ran to him and sat on his knee. They hugged and kissed and lived happily ever after.

In Sarah's version of *The Magic Flute* story, she was responsible for bringing Pamina and Tamino together. She even knew more than the character, Pamina. She explained that Tamino did in fact love her. He was just not allowed to talk to her. Reassured, Pamina was now able to take a tour of Sarah's classroom. Sarah had entered the world of the fictional dream. Talk about feeling powerful—she was in complete control of her characters.

Listening to excerpts from *The Magic Flute* opened up new avenues of response. When we wrote stories about the opera, we listened to "The Queen of the Night." During movement activities, we heard Sarastro's deep voice. The music became part of the children. They could recognize the characters just by hearing the beginning chords of an aria. As Domonique listened to the music of Mozart, she responded in writing to Papageno's bells. This was her draft:

> Papagano ros hes bels
> he mas them Das an Das
> wn h res his bis thea das
>
> *Papageno rings his bells.*
> *He makes them dance and dance.*
> *When he rings his bells, they dance.*

This piece marked a real turning point for Domonique. Though still in the early stages of writing development, she used language so poetically that not only could the class hear the bells, we could even see them dancing.

Dance became an important component of our opera study. Lissy Gulick, our music mentor from the Cleveland Opera, helped us use movement activities to get deeper inside the opera characters. Talking about how evil Monostatos was would not suffice. We had to *become* Monostatos.

"Put Monostatos on your feet," Lissy said. "Keep him in your feet and then put him on your face. Put him in your hands and elbows. Now walk around." Our classroom became filled with grimacing faces and menacing bodies.

The faces and bodies, however, became still when we read various picture book versions of *The Magic Flute*, as well as biographies of the composer. Our students sat wide-eyed watching the taped Glyndebourne Festival Opera production, which used David Hockney's sets. Ingmar Bergman's version, full of whimsy, complete with hot air balloons and visual effects, became a particular favorite of the class. The children's knowledge of *The Magic Flute* story, combined with their familiarity with the music, got them over the hurdle of watching German or Swedish videotapes of the opera. We would stop the tape periodically to make sure the students understood what was going on, but language did not create a barrier. Renata, a child who had watched a friend's copy of the Bergman version over and over again, was beside herself when she received the video as a gift.

Taking advantage of the fact that Oberlin College was about to perform *The Magic Flute*, we made arrangements with Bill Byrnes, the lighting director, for a backstage tour of the set—an experience that transfixed the class. Bill introduced the children to the magic of lighting and special effects on scenery. When the lights on the stage were dark, a full moon appeared. When the house lights came up, the moon disappeared, eliciting oohs and aahs from the enraptured audience. Each new backstage discovery—lush forests that were revealed as flats held up by timber, fire that turned out to be orange lights playing on waving tinfoil—only enhanced the children's appreciation of the technical aspects of theater. Their exclamations of "Wow!" and "Awesome!" were clear indications that they were seeing the magic not in the special effects themselves but in the creativity it took to produce them. The children realized that there were many different ways of envisioning a stage set. With the help of our art teacher, they were eager to design their own scenes from the opera, filling the walls of our room with enormous tempera paintings of wild beasts, chariots, and Queens of the Night.

Senses heightened, they were ready for the final stage of the project: the creation of our own opera. There was a strong sense of purpose as we began the work of choosing a book upon which to base the opera. Finding just the right book proved difficult because the children had so many favorites. Fortunately, there were practical considerations that helped us focus our thinking:

1. It had to be powerful enough to engage our audience.
2. It had to involve our entire class.
3. It had to be short enough to enable us to create and produce our opera in the six weeks that the music mentor would be with us.

After much considered deliberation and negotiation, we all agreed that *The Animal That Drank Up Sound*, written by William Stafford and illustrated by Debra Frasier, was the story we wanted to tell.

For the next six weeks, we worked as composers, librettists, and choreographers. Class meetings took on the feel of an open forum, and the phrase "What if . . ." was often heard. As questions generated other questions, threatening to inundate us, we realized that many of the questions were interrelated. For example, we felt strongly that all of the children should be offered the opportunity of experiencing the on-stage performance aspect of the opera. With a class of forty-two students, the challenge appeared daunting until we thought about it in relation to our question of what to do about sets. We understood the visual impact of scenery. The question was whether we wanted to invest large blocks of our limited time designing sets. Lissy offered an ingenious solution to both problems when she suggested that groups of children act as human sculptures. *They* would be the scenery. Brilliant!

Suddenly our opera had shape. As our class moved through the stages of creating characters, choosing roles, writing lyrics, and composing music, we made some fundamental discoveries about ourselves and our learning. The cooperative efforts that were so much a part of our students' familiar learning environment translated well to the relatively unfamiliar territory of creating lyrics and music for opera. Working together in small groups, they brainstormed dialogue for their characters. Once again, Lissy provided just the right impetus for moving the children forward in their thinking by saying, "Pretend you could sneak up on these characters and listen to their conversation. What might they be saying?" Delighted with the opportunity of engaging in sanctioned eavesdropping, the groups generated lively dialogue.

> I'm intending to catch flies.
> Ribit, ribit, croak. Wow, what a wonderful day!
> What wonderful, juicy flies today.
> What a tasty fly that was.
> Want to play Grab the Mosquito?
> Let's play Leap-Toad and Frog.
> Want to dive?
> What a great day for jumping!
> I'm proud to be an ugly, lumpy toad.
> My warts always get blisters.
> What a happy day.
> I hate to squat all the time because my legs get terrible cramps.

It was fascinating to observe the children as they worked in small groups fine-tuning the dialogue, choosing and discarding words, negotiating with each other and with the adults until they had a song that captured the essence of their character. Carryover from their classroom reading was evident in their use of words like "shrew" (from our study of the Beatrix Potter tales), or plays on words like "I'm very blue about turning brown" (an influence of a study of Jane Yolen's Commander Toad series).

Perhaps the greatest surprise for all of us was the realization that what the children were creating was, in fact, poetry. Here is the song that resulted from the toad dialogue:

> We are proud to be ugly, lumpy toads
> Who keep all the insects away.
> But it does get boring,
> Sitting here catching . . . flies.
> Instead it would be fun to play Leap-Toad
> In the blades of grass.

Our confidence buoyed by the shared experience of creating songs from dialogue, we were ready to compose music for our lyrics. For teachers with no formal musical training, this was the most intimidating phase of the Opera Project. It turned out to be a true learning experience for all those involved. Under the guidance of Lissy Gulick, we did learn simple musical concepts such as beat, measure, and phrasing. That learning was valuable, but even more eye-opening was the way Lissy managed to demystify the process of composing, making it accessible to novices. She helped us visualize whole notes, for example, by explaining them as rubber bands that have to be stretched out. She asked various children to read lines from a song so that we could all hear where the voice naturally pitched high and low and where emphasis was placed. Those highs and lows then became notes on a staff.

She fully understood our emphasis on ownership and would always ask the class to choose from several alternatives. This resulted in some difficult moments for us as teachers when it came time to decide on the beat of particular songs. The rhythm really sets the mood for a piece, and there were times that we had one mood in mind, and the children had a very different idea. For example, the music they wanted to compose for the toad's song seemed to us to be a complete departure from the lyrical mood of the rest of the opera. We had our reservations, but waiting and listening, so vital in our program, became even more important because the children's instincts proved correct. Their comic interpretation provided just the right light touch.

It was also wonderful for the children to realize that all of us were starting out at the same point in this composing business, and they benefited from watching their teachers work through a new learning process right in front of them.

Skill in composition was important, but equally significant were the connections the children made with the rest of their learning. As we worked and reworked melodies, choosing, rearranging, and discarding, several children began to comment that what we were doing was "just like the rough drafts we do in writing." As adults we had been struck by the close parallels between drafting and composing, but it was the playing with words and music that allowed the children to make those same discoveries. Talk about music to a teacher's ears! That type of connection was proof to us that the opera project was providing an environment in which many types of learning were taking place.

From the outset, one of the things that had attracted us to the Cleveland Opera Project was the emphasis on process. The coordinators both at Opera America and Cleveland Opera were very clear that the "create and produce" segment of the project was not to be turned into an extravaganza that would become a school spring program. Emphasis was to be on the *process* of experiencing the many aspects of producing an opera. The concern shared both by project coordinators and by us as teachers committed to discovery learning was that if schools participating in the project began to think of "create and produce" as a performance, adults would feel enormous pressure to take over, and ownership, as well as the sheer joy of mucking about in the world of opera, would be denied the children. Project developers did expect a performance as a way of synthesizing our work, but it was to be of the workshop variety: low-key, in an intimate setting, meant for a small audience.

"Create and produce" was an opportunity for us to extend our classroom community beyond the walls of the school. Although the design of the project originally called for only one opera professional, music mentor Lissy Gulick, it wasn't long before the excitement and infectious spirit of our endeavor drew in some of our parents who had expertise to offer. One child's parents who were professional choreographers worked with the children to develop movement that would enhance the story. A parent who had training in drama helped the children think about their characters. And a parent who is a composer provided a priceless moment. Imagine an award-winning composer premiering his concerto with the Cleveland Orchestra on Thursday and composing with six- and seven-year-olds on Friday. As we observed Ray working his magic with the children, helping them hear the music that was already there within the words, reveling in their insights, it was clear that he was exhibiting his own sense of joy and wonder. He was clearly as excited about the piece he composed with the children as he was with his concerto. Such was the serendipity of this project.

But "create and produce" was also a time that caused us to reflect upon our teaching philosophy. Process oriented though we may be, we found an intriguing phenomenon developing as we approached the date of the performance. A workshop performance had made sense during the initial stages of the project. But as we approached the final week with some songs still to be set to music, choreography changing almost daily as people were struck with new interpretations, everyone began to sense a tension that hadn't existed before. There was more pressure to *finish* things. And the news that both the major funders of the project and the Director of Cleveland Opera were going to be in the audience suddenly created an almost overwhelming desire to turn our workshop into a polished performance. We were torn between our commitment to discovery learning and the desire to have the audience understand that our time had been well spent.

As often happens in the world of primary education, a child offered the insight that brought us back to our real purpose. It was two days before the performance. Judy Ryder, coordinator of the project, and Lissy were discussing with us which songs still needed music. We were feeling a little desperate at the prospect of all that still had to be done when Sarah, the second grader who played our Moon, said very quietly, "I don't think I want my song set to music. It is so sad, that it feels right just to speak it softly." The confidence in that child's voice, the self-assurance that four adult professionals would respect her decision, acted like a magnet to pull us back to our original purpose. This was not about an opera performance for an audience—it was about joy and wonder, discovery and connections, celebration and community. And most of all, it was about children taking charge of their learning. We didn't need a polished performance to tell us that the year had been a valuable one.

The workshop performance did turn out to be extraordinarily exciting. It was very much a *process* performance, but audience members were amazed at the poetry these young children had written, the lyrical quality of the music, and the grace and confidence with which they moved in telling their story.

The Opera Project had several lasting effects that we could not have predicted at the start of the year. It provided an all-encompassing excitement about opera. Besides the students who were borrowing opera tapes from the library, watching their own tapes at home, or listening to opera recordings, our children were attending opera performances. We were happily surprised to discover Russell at a performance of *Pelléas et Mélisande*, an opera we hadn't talked about in school and certainly not one easily accessible to children. His parents said that Russell had given them no choice about attending. Once he learned that an opera was being performed in town, he had to attend.

Studying opera also enlarged our classroom discussions. After reading *Swan Lake* to the class, Micah realized that Siegfried fell in love with the swan Odette as quickly as Tamino fell in love with Pamina. "It's just like Tamino looking at the picture of Pamina," he exclaimed excitedly. Because our study of *The Magic Flute* had given us a common language, everyone in the class knew what Micah was saying. This common language, this knowledge of opera as a form of human expression, helped engender a genuine sense of classroom community. We had all shared similar experiences of creativity and wonderment.

We also discovered that music was a powerful learning tool. It provided one more avenue, one more path in which children could learn to read as well as write. Howard Gardner (1991) observes that education presently focuses mainly on linguistic and logical intelligences. We agree with his argument that "an education built on multiple intelligences can be more effective than one built on just two intelligences. It can develop a broader range of talents, and it can make the standard curriculum accessible to a wider range of students" (81). Music and dance offered another way for the children to respond to the literature we read. The interest in other opera stories like *Aida*, as well as in synopses of ballets such as *Swan Lake*, could be traced to the opera study. Understanding of story sense, the urge to read more stories about opera and write stories relating to opera, were all encouraged by the project. Because we had followed our collective visions and been willing to take risks, we had taken the project in directions the coordinators never envisioned. Everyone was aware that our classroom community had been involved in something very special that would last far beyond the duration of the project. We all knew that music, dance, and opera would be integral parts of our lives.

References

Bergman, Ingmar. 1986. *Ingmar Bergman's The Magic Flute*. Hollywood: Bel Canto Paramount Home Video. Videotape.

Downing, Julie. 1991. *Mozart, Tonight*. New York: Bradbury Press.

Gardner, Howard. 1991. *The Unschooled Mind: How Children Think and How Schools Should Teach.* New York: Basic Books.

Glyndebourne Festival Opera. 1985. *Mozart's The Magic Flute.* New York, NY: Video Arts International. Videotape.

Greaves, Margaret. 1989. *Magic Flute: The Story of Mozart's Opera.* Henry Holt.

Isadora, Rachel. 1991. *Swan Lake.* New York: G. P. Putnam.

Opera America. 1990. *Music! Words! Opera!* Washington, DC: MMB Music.

Price, Leontyne. 1990. *Aida.* San Diego, CA: Harcourt, Brace, Jovanovich.

Sabin, Francene. 1990. *Mozart, Young Musical Genius.* Mahwah, New Jersey: Troll.

Stafford, William. 1992. *The Animal that Drank Up Sound.* San Diego, CA: Harcourt, Brace, Jovanovich.

Weil, Lisl. 1991. *Wolferl.* New York: Holiday House.

FROM WRITERS' WORKSHOP TO ARTISTS' WORKSHOP: EXPANDING MEANINGS THROUGH WORDS AND PICTURES

KAREN ERNST
Westport, CT Public Schools

*T*he room was silent as the students' eyes glanced from a picture they had selected from their portfolio to the gray folders holding the white paper of their artist's notebooks. I had asked a class of fourth graders what they saw in the picture, what they felt as they looked, what title they would give the piece (Figure 1).

Hands went up after several minutes as students wanted to share (Figure 2). Renee read from her artist's notebook, words describing a torn paper collage in her portfolio: "Title black hole: spacey, colorful, confetti, unpieced crayon, gold rush?, mountains, unmade shapes." Her list led to a work where words and pictures worked together to express meaning.

Black Hole

See and create
Watch and create
Work toward an ending of confetti
To describe it
Watch a gold rush
    or unpiece a crayon
Each is a work of art

131

Figure 1

Bit of space
    scraps of paper
Make up shapes
    Use unmade ones
Try a masterpiece
    You're an artist

After doing a careful line drawing of a pot of geraniums, (Figure 3) Allen wrote, "It is easier to write about something you

Figure 2

We paint what
we see...
not what
we know.

see with your eyes. If I drew a picture, I could express my
feelings of that picture much easier." Here, pictures led to words.
As in Renee and Allen's work, both visual and written expression
gave students ways to express their uniqueness, their creative
thought, thereby widening their abilities to say what they meant.
Paul Connolly (1990), Director of the Institute for Writing and
Thinking at Bard College, suggests both drawing and writing liber-
ate a student's thinking, intelligence, and ability to see. Writing

Figure 3

gave Renee freedom to use a "tentative language" (7) that helped her describe what she saw in her collage. Allen's words began to describe the ways pictures helped him make meaning. In our artists' workshop, parallel to my former writers' workshop, students experienced a community of learning where reading, writing, and picture making worked together to help them learn, think, express themselves, and make meaning.

For twenty-two years I taught eighth graders and was influenced by the writers' workshop approach of Atwell (1987), Graves (1983), and Calkins (1986). As a result of declining enrollment, low seniority in the district, and holding an art certification, I was assigned to a new position of teaching art in an elementary school. During this year I was teacher, learner, participant, observer, artist, and writer with my new students.

My role included questioning my students about their learning and changing my classroom based on my on-going inquiry. This new workshop was influenced by my former eighth graders' excited inquiry about learning, writing, and reading. I was a stranger to the elementary classroom, a stranger to the art curriculum, but no stranger to teacher research, teaching, children, learning, and the arts as a way of making meaning. Intricate to the story of this emerging workshop are the words and pictures of my students and of me as well, as I used drawing and writing as a means for observing and understanding my students at work (Figure 4).

The Vision: An Artists' Workshop
Parallel to a Writers' Workshop

Third graders entered the room, followed the directions on the easel, and sat on the rug by the red house banner in the area marked "SHARING." Our workshop began with a rehearsal for learning; on this day I displayed a work by Kandinsky, thinking it would excite them to visit a small exhibit of the artist's original work at a local gallery. In our daily rehearsal we looked at art to understand what real artists do, at illustrations to see how words and pictures work together. We listened to stories to help inspire and encourage students to open their imaginations. In our rehearsal in writers' workshop we sat in a circle, wrote together, shared our writing, read works of authors, and learned to listen to each other. In both work-

Figure 4

Chelsea in black and green, pencil and crayons, drawing Zuckerman's Farm... in *Charlotte's Web*.

shops, as we shared student work or that of artists, I knew that this would help build a community of learners, help students learn to discuss art and literature, and provide them with ideas for their own work.

I asked the class to tell me what media or what topic they would use for their pictures. I watched with anticipation as everyone got their materials and went to work. Self-selecting topics for writing and books for reading in the writers' workshop led me to encourage students to select their own topics for picturing, drawing, painting, and pasting. Probing the students' opinions and allowing them to choose moved me toward focusing on student choice.

Writing was a choice some students made during their one hour in art. As one student painted, I sat with him and brainstormed a list of words inspired by his picture. Emma worked on a collage series, prompted by poems she had written in her classroom upstairs (Figure 5).

My note taking in my research journal and record keeping began to help me know what we would do next, and as students made choices in painting, collage, writing, and mixing media, they showed me possibilities beyond what I proposed. I sat next to my students while they worked, feeling less the need to watch over or direct them than moved to question what they were making, what inspired them, constantly noting the stories that were embedded in the pictures they created.

Evaluation and assessment were on-going, propelled by student choice and my role as an observer. As in my writers' workshop, I did not grade individual pieces of writing or pictures or keep a grade book with quiz scores and numbers. Instead, I kept a chart with a narrative on each student's progress, evidence of our conferences, my questioning, observations, our shared learning, their published writing, and pieces in progress. In the artists' workshop I recorded topics for pictures, attempts in using new media, or stories connected with their pictures. Whole class response to work led to personal reflection and on-going evaluation and stimulated students to engage in their own projects, not those assigned by me.

In both workshops students kept all of their work in portfolios, including mistakes and plans for stories and pictures. Students were discouraged from throwing away work. I emphasized that artists learn from their mistakes and later often use sketches, ideas, or starts found in their portfolios. The valuable learning I gained from the end-of-quarter conference in the writers' workshop led me to create a portfolio review in the artists' workshop. Students reviewed their portfolios with their parents, guided by questions I sent home: Tell me about some of your pictures; How did you make them? Which picture do you like best? Why? Where do you get your ideas in the artists' workshop? Through these reviews I learned that students were influenced by experiences they had, books they read, and mostly by other students.

Collaboration among students in both workshops was important. Just as students in the writers' workshop met in peer groups to confer over writing and get responses to works in progress, students in the artists' workshop sat at tables together discussing their work and sharing their processes of picture making. In writers' workshop students shared unfinished pieces with the class and published their writing for a wider audience in the hallway outside of the classroom. Similarly, in the artists' workshop, pictures were shared in the rehearsal on the rug, and the work informed a wider audience of parents, teachers, and other students when students displayed pictures and words in the all-school exhibitions in the hallways. Publishing and exhibiting extended the collaboration and learning.

The opening exhibition of children's work, on display in the hallways, stimulated the work in the artists' workshop. Students immediately began selecting possible pictures from their portfolios for the next exhibition. They mounted their works on colored construction paper at The Frame Shop, a corner of the studio with stacks of colored construction paper, paper cutter, staplers, and glue. As students selected work from their portfolios for the publishing board in the writers' workshop or the hallway exhibitions in the artists' workshop, they were involved in self-assessment. The decision to go public propelled their work forward. Four times throughout the year the hallways of the school became a gallery as some work of each student was exhibited. A poster announced the exhibit and text panels throughout the exhibition described the workshop process and included student writing.

Writing about the process of thinking and learning was essential in both workshops. In writers' workshop students wrote about their writing process, used writing to rehearse for further writing, wrote letters to each other about independent reading, and developed essays that evolved from personal dialogue with literature. In artists' workshop students recorded their thinking in their artist's notebooks. They wrote about their picture making,

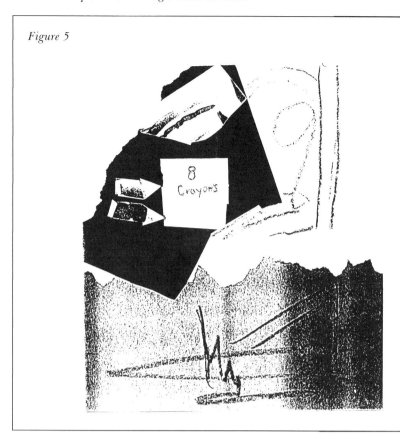

Figure 5

wrote about their process, used writing to express meanings in their picture, and wrote letters about the pictures exhibited in the hallways. Writing in both workshops helped the community develop through reading written thoughts aloud.

Through writing and reading with my eighth-grade students I not only modeled for them but learned with them how to be a better reader and writer. In the Artists' Workshop, I continued to be part of the community of learners. When my young students wrote I wrote with them, sharing my thoughts, my new learning. As the workshop emerged closer to my "vision," their work as inquiring artists inspired me to engage in my own inquiry as an artist, pushing the margins of my own creativity as I worked with the same materials as my students. They helped me move beyond only drawing in my journal, to begin experimenting with

Brilliant, dull
Pink Turquoise and
Gray, crayons are
made to make the
world shine all
day, that's how the
rain goes away

crayon and watercolor, or capturing images of students with paint and pen.

I worked and learned with my eighth-grade students, but there were times when I pulled back. Observation also played a key role in this emerging artists' workshop, in my learning about my new, younger students, and about the role of arts in literacy. I made myself an observer of the workshop at work, raising questions with my students: What is the relationship between a writers' workshop approach and an artists' workshop? How do I achieve a balance between providing choice and giving direction? How does literature, art, portfolio, exhibition fit in? What importance do students place on my work as an artist and learner? What happens when writing is an integral part of the art experience? The process of reflecting made me constantly revise and refine the workshop to reach toward my vision and to include new learning from my students, their projects, goals, and needs.

Nancie Atwell (1990) describes a workshop of learning as one "in which writing and reading are learned in the richest possible context and appreciated as tools of the highest quality for helping children come to know about the world" (xxii). In the artists' workshop I wanted to provide the richest possible context to bring the arts into whole learning, to make it a partner with reading and writing. Ruth Hubbard (1989) in examining the complementary processes of drawing and writing in a first-grade classroom writes, "Pictures as well as words are important to human beings in their communication; we need to expand our narrow definition of literacy to include visual dimensions, and in so doing answer the call of researchers for the recognition of multi-literacies and ways these literacies can work to complement each other" (150). In this workshop we did not limit ourselves to what pictures looked like; we explored what thinking went into making art and used writing as a powerful tool to help us make sense of experience.

The Artist's Notebooks: Answers, Inquiries, Meanings

All third and fourth graders kept artist's notebooks, recording in them their process, discoveries, and thinking. They used the notebooks to develop ideas, sketch plans, and think about meanings in their pictures. Vera John-Steiner (1985), in her study of the processes of "experienced thinkers," found that "it is by means of language that poets, writers, and philosophers, who are driven by the need to think beyond the limits of the known, have attempted to share with others their personal inquiries" (111). In my workshop it was through writing that students explored and shared with me their personal inquires.

As students balanced on their stools in the classroom studio, their gray folders opened in front of them, they initially wrote in response to questions I posed (Figure 6): What did you discover? What is your picture about? What do you plan to make? One boy wrote, "I learned the more I was making the picture the more it became different." "An alligator pattern," was the response from another student. "I need to finish my cutting picture." Others, like Matt, expressed a sense of real accomplishment. "Today the teacher framed my picture with orange paper. The teacher also said I need a poem for my spatter painting." Writing revealed the thinking, planning,

Figure 6

and discovering that occurred in their process of making pictures.

Through writing I began to understand what was inside the spattered picture, the pages of scribble, the bold strokes of color. Writing helped me see that there was more going on here than just making pictures. Robbie wrote in his artist's notebook, "Today i had a grat ecsperience. I finished my mask and got to do a painting, mixed new colors and art has been good to me." As Emma leaned over next to me just before her classmates shared their writing, she whispered, "I wrote a whole page."

Through continuous sharing of student work, her classmates and I learned the secrets and surprises within the on-going work. Writing together helped us work as authentic learners, using writing to help think about what pictures meant. Carl wrote, "I think my picture looks like a river with a bridge and a sunset behind a mountain." Others wrote about the process of making art. "I just ripped paper, making more things with ripping the paper." I learned what inspired them, from books they were reading to their thoughts and personal experience. Students described what they learned and accomplished: "I learned that when you're making a collage and you overlap you can make neat and weird shapes."

Kindergarteners through second graders described their discoveries as I recorded their thoughts on a large newsprint sketch pad, our community artists' notebook. They described that "colors change to other colors," or "Emma and I have been asking each other what we want to make." This form of writing showed that their work, just as that of the older students, included invention, surprise, collaboration, and more. The combination of writing and pictures evident in the classroom led them to begin asking me to write their stories on their pictures as they worked.

By making writing an essential element in the workshop, the intention was not only to allow students to draw or picture as they learned how to write but to encourage both visual and verbal expression. Writing helped students think about what they were making and what they planned to make thus moving them to come to the workshop ready to choose their own projects. For some students writing in their artist's notebooks, became a necessary form of note taking, helping them remember where they were as projects began carrying from one week to the next. One boy asked, "Can I write it [his collage] down so I don't forget where I am?" Connolly (1990) describes specifically how writing is essential in an art classroom: "In the art studio itself, such writing can assist discovery when words are used to invert conventional figure/ground relationships and allow new figures of thought to emerge upon new grounds of language". (4). Through my students' writing, I learned ways writing was used. Their writing revealed their on-going inquiries and meanings.

I began to see evidence that students could come to the workshop with their projects and ideas. My role was to provide them with literature, art, and technique as they moved forward. With the possibility of writing always there and encouraged, students began to use it as a tool in their work in the classroom revealing more about their process of thinking and creating. Writing sharpened students' ability to look at and consider what they saw in their own pictures. In her first entry Eileen wrote: "I would call my first picture blue mountain and golden river. I just kept tearing out pieces and never thought about it until I was finished and I really looked at it. I could see a blue mountain and a golden river. It really didn't change like I said I really didn't think about it." Without writing, meanings would have been private; students would have focused on the appearance of pictures or on my interpretations. Anthony was able to describe in writing how looking was an important act in making pictures: "It [writing] helped me see that even though you might make something that you don't like you can change it and make it something you do like."

Writing as a Form of Assessment

The act of writing and the emphasis on thinking—not on the way pictures looked—helped students acquire the tools of close observation, use their imagination, describe their own process, and importantly, assess their own work. As Thomas described it, "I really like art writing. I like thinking and writing about my art." He often made designs, and writing helped him assess what he was doing and even though he was dissatisfied with his pictures he was able to describe how he wanted to change as an artist:

> Today I drew three pictures. Two were very weird, one looked like a sleigh with wheels, the other was a shack. My last one I hate. It's all sloppy and boring. . . . I think I made too many designs and should start making more real things, like a forest or a town or a city. Next time I might do something like that.

Emma concluded, "If I could be more interested in imagination, I think I could be a better artist." Sandy described how she was learning to look and think about her work in a new way, "Now I study it and put myself in it and I think how I like it in my picture."

Writing helped students revise their pictures. Ellen's painting of trees and a pond had inspired many students in other grades to try their own versions, but the task of describing her process of making the picture in writing seemed difficult. Ellen wrote, then sketched her painting into her notebook, (Figure 7) saying she had forgotten something in her painting. Unpinning her painting from the board, she returned to the work table, adding the reflection of the trees in the pond. Writing and sketching in her notebook helped her revise her picture, linking the complementary processes in an important way.

Writing in our artists' workshop—in any subject, in any workshop of learning—intensified thinking, led to forming new ideas, and helped me understand interpretations. As Ann Berthoff

Figure 7

(1984) writes, "An understanding of interpretation can help all teachers see the virtue of claiming that writing is a mode of learning and a way of knowing" (165). Writing was a critical part of the artists' workshop. It helped students see, think, say, sort out, understand, and imagine. Students began using writing and picture making separately and together to express themselves. Jake wrote: "I've become a better writer and that writing goes to my pictures. I think I've become better at drawing and painting.

I've learned how to mix more colors. I've learned how to look at pictures more closely and the feeling of that picture." Writing and picturing were forms of meaning making, and by introducing writing as a key element in the workshop, pictures and words worked together as complementary processes of knowing, providing a link between words and images as forming processes. Students here used writing, looking, and making pictures, together and recursively, to shape and form their thinking.

Writing as Art: Art as Writing

At times students described art as writing and writing as art. Emma wrote, "My whole writing time was spent looking at different poses of a horse." Laurent wrote in his notebook, "In art you don't just write a piece of art and then say you're done. First you imagine what you're going to make, then imagine where you are going to put the colors. Then when you're finished drawing, you see how much better your painting is when you imagine." In the artists' workshop students were writing pieces of art and turning writing into art.

As questions surfaced about the emerging workshop, about the connections between writing and images, student writing informed me about how painting and making pictures were a true form of expression. "I can express myself with paintings. Paintings are the only way to be truthful about how you feel inside and what you're really like," wrote Martin. Painting led to feelings of self-confidence. "I feel good as a painter it makes all my feelings shine through. I think painting is just another form of words . . . when I paint I feel good all over. When I am painting I feel important. I may not be very good at it but I still like it anyways."

Pictures led to words and the words revealed meanings, adding to the power behind the pictures. For example, Anthony wrote about making two paintings: "When I was painting, I felt happy. The colors streamed from my mind and each color had a meaning to be in the picture. Then when I was drawing I felt like I was climbing the mountains and my cabin was down below. The fresh air was in my lungs. It made me feel happy." Just as pictures led to words, words led to pictures.

"Writing," Martin called out as I took an assessment of what my students planned to work on. Writing became one of the art forms, as some students spent their one hour in art working on a poem or a story. Martin and a friend, who even asked to come during their recess, worked on their poems then created pictures.

A Momentary Rush of Water on the Rio Grande
I feel a smooth cool draft of air.
Space, open space. All I see . . . a dam.
Then suddenly water rushing violently on and on.
Never stopping. But only for a moment.

Just as Emma had brought her poems from her writers' workshop to inspire her collage, a third grader's choice of a project in the artists' workshop was influenced by his new learning in his classroom in metaphor and simile. Two fourth-grade girls asked if they could "write poems" before they "did art."

Jonathan turned his feelings into words and his words into art when he wrote: "It felt wild, wacky. It felt like a splash or colors. It felt strange, cold, warm. It felt different. Scary. It felt great. It felt like magic." (Figure 8). For Renee, Jonathan, and others, pictures and the act of making, along with the use of writing, led to poetic, expressive writing. When words and pictures were available and valued as ways of expression, the experiences of learning in our workshop were made in bold strokes of words, and in crafted lines of color. Words helped describe the valuable role of pictures in the students' evolving literacy.

Endings of Confetti

"I think that shapes and color show more than words. I can see world beyond world. I see bat, and caves, triangles, line, repeats and unrepeats," wrote Dennis. Making and looking at pictures were simultaneous processes, and for students like Dennis, or Martin, paintings and pictures were the best way to express themselves. Words helped them express ideas and helped me understand the value of the visual as a way of knowing. Sondra, on the other hand, wrote, "Art is very important. It gives me ideas for what to write about that's important. It makes my imagination grow. . . . It lets me find and express my feelings." In the artists' workshop writing and making pictures were partners, forms of discovery, ways of thinking, means of expression, and both were art forms. Myra Barrs (1988), through her work at The Center for Language in Primary Education in London, states that writing is "in some important way bound up with picturing, and the child's meanings are located in a combination of picture and text with no clean boundary between them" (58).

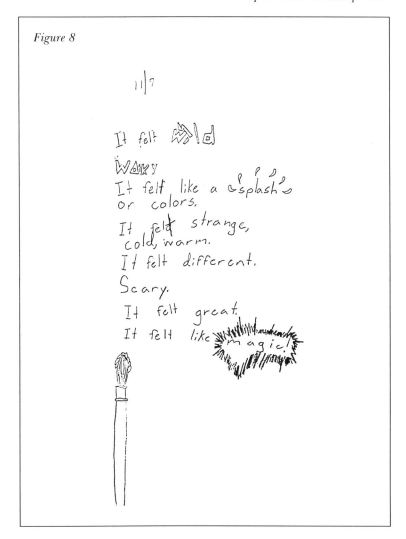

Figure 8

Art led to writing, writing led to pictures, and both were valued and used together in helping students use their imaginations. Students were spilling words onto the page, "unpiecing crayons, working toward endings of confetti," expressing through words and pictures, describing their way of seeing and interpreting in more ways than I had imagined.

References

Atwell, Nancie, ed. 1990. *Coming to Know: Writing to Learn in the Intermediate Grades.* Portsmouth, NH: Heinemann.

————. (1987). *In the middle: Writing, Reading, and Learning with Adolescents.* Portsmouth, NH: Boynton/Cook.

Barrs, Myra. 1988. Drawing a Story: Transitions between Drawing and Writing. In M. Lightfoot and N. Martin (Eds.), *The Word for Teaching Is Learning: Essays for James Britton* (pp. 51–69). Portsmouth, NH: Heinemann.

Berthoff, Ann, ed. 1984. *Reclaiming the Imagination: Philosophical Perspectives for Writers and Teachers of Writing.* Portsmouth, NH: Boynton/ Cook.

Calkins, Lucy. (1986). *The Art of Teaching Writing.* Portsmouth, NH: Heinemann.

Coles, Robert. 1989. *The Call of Stories: Teaching and the Moral Imagination.* Boston: Houghton Mifflin.

Connolly, Paul. 1990. "Writing to See: The Languages of Visual Thinking." *Art and Academe 2*, 1–9.

Graves, Donald. 1983. *Writing: Teachers and Children at Work.* Portsmouth, NH: Heinemann.

Hubbard, Ruth. 1989. *Authors of Pictures, Draughtsmen of Words.* Portsmouth, NH: Heinemann.

John-Steiner, Vera. 1985. *Notebooks of the Mind: Explorations of Thinking.* New York: Harper & Row.

THE MIND'S EAR

LISA LENZ
University of New Hampshire

*O*ne cold winter night in 1991, I sat in a crowded auditorium at the 92nd Street Y in New York City waiting to hear the poet Denise Levertov read her work aloud. I'd come to the reading— the first formal poetry reading I'd ever attended—knowing that I liked Levertov's poetry but uncertain about what to expect of the event itself. I half expected to find myself surrounded by an audience of snooty insiders who understood every nuance of what was being read while I sat there, baffled.

Instead, I found myself among people who looked as if they, too, might have hurried to get there after work. Briefcases were tucked underneath chairs and heavy coats removed and smoothed into place over chairbacks whenever someone found a place to sit. But most of the people seated around me also seemed to be shedding their after-work fatigue, replacing it with a sense of anticipation that intrigued me.

When Levertov began to read, I understood what their excitement had been about. The beauty of the language was overwhelming. We sat transfixed by the subtle chemistry of sound and sense in her poetry for most of the evening. When I returned home, I sat re-reading her poems until well past midnight, hearing them and wondering how Levertov had learned to play with the sound of language.

The next day, when I told the children in my class about the way Levertov's reading had made me feel, they knew exactly what I was talking about. We'd just begun a nine-week poetry project, which had been inspired by a seven-year-old child's magical reading of e. e. cummings' poem, "hist whist." By inviting her listeners into her experience of a poem, Jill, like Denise Levertov, had managed to enchant us all. Their readings helped me to recognize how little attention I'd paid to the talents of children who needed to throw themselves into publishing that went beyond print.

The love for the sheer aural beauty of language that Jill evoked in her classmates was never a part of the grade school experience when I was a child. Our voices were, in almost every sense, missing from our classrooms. The spoken word was treated as an unwieldy source of potential energy that simmered just below the surface of every classroom, a force that teachers attempted to cap. Students responded to questions posed, went through the torture of once-a-year oral reports, and asked each other furtive questions about what to do.

Inside the quiet of those rooms, there were no low-risk ways of rehearsing ideas through conversation or hearing our own voices play with the creation of character whenever we read aloud. Children read aloud, but it was never because they enjoyed the experience. Teachers made them do it and used their performance as a means of assessing their ability to decode. In spite of the obstacles in their path, a handful of extroverts always managed to make themselves heard. But the majority of students were like me, unlikely to take risks or rehearse when the stakes were so high and our silence left so unchallenged.

Luckily, I grew up listening to both my parents read aloud and learned to love the sounds of language through them. My mother sang to us and my father, who made up the stories he told, loved to play with the sound of each character's voice. I could never quite create the same effect when I read aloud, but whenever I curled up with a book, I listened to the rhythm of its words.

This aesthetic facet of a reader's interaction with her text seldom receives its fair share of attention in schools. Yet the role it plays in a child's development as both a reader and a writer is crucial. Eudora Welty (1984) described the phenomenon and it's importance in her memoir, *One Writer's Beginnings*.

> It isn't my mother's voice, or the voice of any person I can identify, certainly not my own. It is human, but inward, and it is inwardly that I listen to it. It is to me the voice of the story or the poem itself. The cadence, whatever it is that asks you to believe, the feeling that resides in the printed word, reaches me through the reader-voice. I have supposed, but never found out, that this is the case with all readers—

to read as listeners—and with all writers, to write as listeners. It may be part of the desire to write. (11–12)

Learning to hear that voice—the voice of the text—may also be part of the desire to read. But we often spend so much instructional time wondering whether our students have grasped the sense of the written word that we neglect to help them relish the beauty of its sound. We treat one of reading's chief pleasures as a mere by-product of the process and inadvertantly deny our students the chance to learn to savor the sound of language in the pieces they write themselves.

The poetry project let my class begin to revel in language. Fortunately, our room was already filled with some types of poetry. Every morning since September, the children had gathered on the rug for twenty minutes of singing favorite songs and reading poems from the tattered homemade folders they called their Jingle Books. And I'd often begun story time with a poem or two from an anthology. But when I listened closely, I noticed that the strongest poetry in our room was rooted in what the children said.

Six- and seven-year-olds describe the world in ways older poets would envy. They're eager to explore and describe but are far too young to have adopted either the conventions of adult speech or an older child's concern over what his or her peers might think. To get them to attend to the presence of poetry in each others' everyday speech, I set aside eight feet of blackboard two weeks before our project began and labelled it "Sounds Like Poetry." Then, whenever a child said something that sounded particularly poetic, I made a point of noticing it and added the comment to the board.

> Candace, describing stars:
> *Little white specks that drift across the sky.* . . .

> Michael, describing ideas found in old notebook entries:
> *It's like sparks from a campfire. They're not quite burning*
> *yet, but they could start a fire anytime.*

> Steven, describing wrinkles:
> *Wrinkles, like branches in someone's cheek.* . . .

The children were quick to adopt my role and began listening to each other with an intensity I hadn't seen before. By the time the project began, they walked into the room convinced that they were poets.

An uninterrupted, two-hour block of time each morning allowed me free reign to shape the immersion experience. We began the project by focusing for three weeks on what the children called "other people's poetry." Each morning, after their Jingle Books were collected, the children ran to get pencils and high-lighter markers while I passed out the copies of the poems we were about to read together. While I read, the children listened intently and then told me which was their favorite. We then returned to that poem and read it aloud together several times. The children marked up their individual copies to show which words or lines had struck them.

We followed our readings with what Jerome Haste calls a "say something": each child turned to one or two others and took a moment to tell what they'd noticed. Afterwards, we shared our reactions in a whole group circle. I'd also respond to the poem, offering my personal reaction first to a partner and later in the circle when my turn came. The children went on to write and draw about their reactions to the poems and made other entries in their notebooks while I conferenced with individuals.

At first, their reactions were one-dimensional. They'd mention a certain word from the poem that had caught their attention or drew an image it had made them see. In Figure 1, Rehana is taken with the expression "eat-me-red" in the third line of Joanne Ryder's "Poem."

As their experience with poetry deepened so did their reactions. Children often began by describing an event from their own lives that connected to a poem but would then go on to notice the poet's choice of words, the shape of a poem, or a sound that repeated. Just before we read Nan Fry's poem, "Apple," the children played outdoors in the snowy schoolyard. Six-year-old Meghan then responded to the poem by writing, "I see a half of an apple with the skin as the red sky, the white as the snow, and the seeds as the star, and someone is eating an apple and walking through snow, and I hear 'crunch, crunch.' "

After three weeks of immersion in poetry as readers, speakers, and listeners, the children began to write poems of their own. The spillover effect was mind-boggling. Powerful images, careful word choices, repetitions, and a sense of playfulness with line breaks and shape appeared again and again in their work. By sharing their poems with each other, the children grew more aware of how they'd crafted each piece.

Their lack of self-consciousness made it possible for them to say things in ways that older children might have shied away

Figure 1

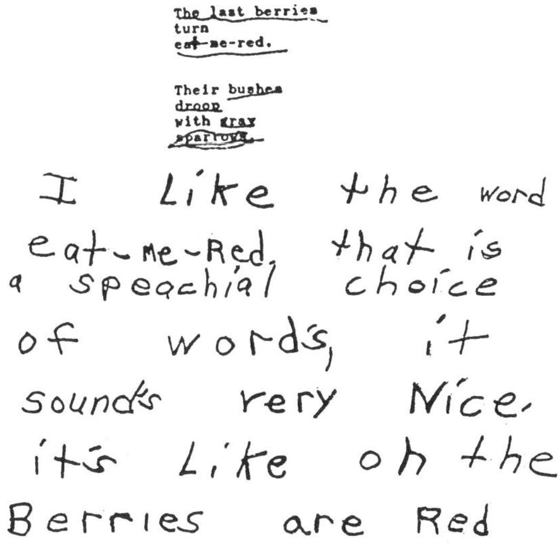

The_last berries_
turn
eat—me-red.

Their bushes
droop
with gray
sparrows

$\mathcal{I}$ Like the word
eat—me—Red, that is
a speachial choice
of words, it
sounds rery Nice.
its Like oh the
Berries are Red

from. Their poems most often sprang either from observations they made during the day or from old notebook entries. One day, six-year-old Meghan stood quietly watching the snow fall outside our classroom window before she suddenly began to write in her notebook. What I thought might be an entry turned out to be a poem.

When she shared "Snow" with the class, Meghan explained how the words on the white page had "started to look like the flakes of snow in the sky, like they really were" when she was in the midst of writing her poem. (See Figure 2.) The children, who'd grown comfortable talking about how poets made use of white space, responded appreciatively. I was stunned. Not only had she captured the image of the featherly clusters of snow that had drifted past our window. She'd also captured the stillness of that afternoon and had wrapped her poem in the gentle mood of a lullaby.

Rehana's poem, "Sun," occurred to her as she was checking

Figure 2

Sno foling Sno foling

all wrld arad the

Sno foling Sno foling

all wrld arad the

the Sno an d boing
the wind our
A lalbiy

on the growth of the radishes we'd planted in a box next to the
window. While she was writing, she happened to glance up at
the windowsill where I'd taped a copy of Karla Kuskin's poem,
"Radish." Rehana read the poem and laughed at the suggestion
that poets ought to write about radishes instead of about the
moon. Because she shared Kuskin's sense of playfulness, Rehana
wrote her poem "Sun" as a parody of "Radish" and decided to
send an illustrated copy of it to Kuskin. (See Figure 3.) She spent

Figure 3

days working on the border, an alternating pattern of the sun, radishes, and crescent moons, but her work paid off. Kuskin was delighted with the poem and promptly wrote back to her.

The children's ability to frame their experience with unique imagery continued long after the project was over. When the first crop of dandelions went to seed in the yard outside our window, the children were anxious to send them flying. One of the children returned from recess and quietly wrote a poem he called "Dandelion Weeds."

Dandelion Weeds
by
Michael Ciccone

They are weeds, not what you want,
but nice little flowers only an inch across.
They close up to die, opening puffy-soft
to spread seeds across a field,
little parachuters.

Poems also grew out of the subjects that appeared time after time in our notebook entries, as if demanding our attention. One week, the children weren't surprised to hear me say that I was working on a poem about my older sister; they knew I'd been making notebook entries about her for several days. The draft of the poem I shared with them was triggered by a memory of the two of us racing through the house when we were both very young. I told the children how I was struggling to bring that feeling of running into the pace of the poem. The children listened and told me which parts made them feel that pace and which parts did not.

The next day, Jason wrote a poem about his pet guinea pig, Ginger, who was apparently as fond of racing as were my sister and I. When he read his poem to the class, he told them that he was trying to make the lines of his poem race, too. We thought he did. I later copied Jason's poem onto poster paper so he could tell the class about how he'd decided on the line breaks he'd made.

Ginger
by
Jason Desch

Ginger,
Ginger, fast-as-a-lightning-bolt Ginger
gets out of his cage
at night and runs all night
and in the morning
goes back to his cage,
slams the door
and goes back to sleep,
and in the night,
he does it
again.

Young children are often able to write about what makes them feel angry or afraid without censoring their thoughts. Many of my students wrote about their fear of losing a pet or their grief over a pet's death. When they did, their listeners noticed aspects of the way their poems were crafted before they did; for them, the poem was pure, distilled emotion.

Rehana was surprised when her listeners pointed out the internal rhymes she used in "My Cat." Meghan had no idea how strongly her listeners would react to the last line of "My Thoughts." But as they grew more aware of how they worked and made more purposeful use of certain tools in their writing, the children never let technical skills become the starting point of a poem.

My Cat
by Rehana Lanewala

When the time
has come
for my cat to
die I
will
droop
while
other flowers
bloom.

My Thoughts
by Meghan Shapiro

I thought
and thought,
"When am I going to die?"
because my dog died
and my heart fainted away.

Some children wrote poems as a way of responding to someone else's poem. Occasionally, a child's poem would mirror the form of one of his or her favorite poems, but the heart of what was said was always rooted in that child's own life.

"The Rain"
by
Jennifer Kinsey

The rain is dropping on you,
tapping on the ground
and singing to you,
pouring on you
tap
    tap
      tap
making puddles like pools
on the sidewalks,
tapping on the roof
like a little song,
like you're waking up in the morning
with the sun tapping
on your head.

Poem
by
Chris Stephanelli
I loved my grandpa.
He died.
It was like I lost a part of myself.
There's nothing more to say.
The poem ends,
Soft as it began—
I loved my grandpa.

Soon after the children began to write their own poems, I noticed that something unusual was happening during writing workshop. At first, I couldn't quite put my finger on what it was. Then I realized that many of the children were re-reading their poems, saying them to themselves as they wrote, as if listening to the sound of it all had become part of their writing process. It was as if they'd developed as sense of audience that began with themselves. One child, six-year-old Erin, was able to comment and reflect on this habit.

> I pretend I'm that person who really pays attention to me and then I say to myself what I think they might say. I sort of read it silently to myself and say, "Well, I think this was good, but I think I need to change this part." And then I read it the regular way to a real kid and then I read it the changed way. With "The Library," I put "fairies bring *kids* to their hiding places" and "kids" sounds really tacky. It doesn't sound like the fairytale way I want it to sound, so I changed it [to *children*].

Other reasons for saying poems aloud as part of the writing process soon emerged. One child who'd had an unusually difficult time with print because of the reversals he saw was an articulate, sensitive speaker. He wanted to write a poem about his dog, Mickey, but the mechanics of doing so had stood in his way. We worked out a partnership that other pairs in the class later adopted and nicknamed "Write That Down." Mike talked about Mickey while I wrote down what he said. After a minute or two of meandering talk, he began to tell me the story of the day his dog nearly drowned. Later, as I re-read what he'd said, he highlighted the lines that seemed as if they might be the seeds of a poem.

When I re-read those lines with him one more time, he suddenly began to say them in an entirely new order, adding and subtracting parts as if zeroing in on the most important part of the story. I wrote down what he said and later he shared the poem with the class.

My Dog Mickey
by
Mike C.

My dog Mickey was trying to swim.
He was lying at the bottom
of the pool, moving his paws.
I dove in and got him—
He was only five pounds.
There was stuff in his mouth—
old leaves and pricker branches.
He was bleeding a little.

He shook himself dry
and did not die.

Several of the other children also knew what it was like to love an animal and come so close to losing it. They were moved by his poem and let him know it. Mike beamed and responded quietly to their comments.

When print is an obstacle for children, it's easy for them to make discouraging comparisons between their own writing and that of their peers. They decline chances to share their work and allow their own voices to fall out of writing workshops. But many of these children are able to compose their stories aloud. I needed to find a way of honoring Mike's abilities in oral language and remind myself of the shortcomings of a workshop culture where access to the attention of an audience is limited to those who find it easy to work with print.

Another child who needed to say his poem aloud as he wrote it had completely different needs. Instead of making any other sort of entry in his notebook, Chris had been drawing numerous versions of a fierce-looking knight for days. Whenever I'd asked about him, Chris had responded vaguely. It was just something he'd started to draw, something that fascinated him. I felt torn between wishing that he'd get busy and write something and realizing that he was in the grips of a good idea that simply hadn't fleshed out yet.

Then I decided that Chris probably had something to teach me. I approached him again, and when I asked Chris what the knight's name was, something clicked. He took a quick look at the diamond-shaped shield he'd drawn and told me that his character was called "The Kiteman."

Chris is particularly adept at creating stories off-the-cuff. He also has a tremendous sense of audience appeal. So when I asked him to join me in modeling a partners' conference before the class, I knew what sort of opportunity I was dropping in his lap. During our conference, I pointed to the blood dripping off The Kiteman's sword and asked what his character had been up to. Chris looked at his audience, turned to me, and began to invent. The Kiteman, it seemed, was a notorious creature with a thousand gory deeds to his name. When Chris finished telling me about the worst of them, I told him that his knight sounded exactly like the kind of ne'er-do-well that was the stuff of legends and story poems.

Chris knew how much the class loved story poems. He'd memorized five of them himself. "The Kiteman came from . . . ," he paused, trying to think of the name of a place. "Kilimanjaro?" I suggested, but he shook his head. "No . . . The Kiteman came from Kitmandee," he began and drank in the approving glances of his friends.

Minutes later, he was tapping out a rhythm on a table and jotting down lines. He shared the first verse of his poem with the class later that morning and the response he got made him finish the rest of it quickly. Every line was said aloud before it was written. Chris explained his writing process in a subsequent conference.

The Kiteman
by

Chris Stephanelli

The Kiteman came from Kitmandee
And wandered through the woods.
He came across a helpless man
And killed him where he stood.

He came across a quiet town
And came across its school.
He went straight to the principal
And killed the ugly fool.

Then he turned and roared a fearless roar
And everybody ran.
They hid inside a deep, dark woods
And were not seen again.

But then he met the boldest knight—
They fought and fought and fought.
And The Kiteman was no more—
He deserved just what he got.

Chris' conference notes:

I heard "**da dala da dala dala**" and I came up with the rest of my story poem from the beat and rhyming. And I also talked out loud to hear the beat. I said, "**da dala da dala dala**" for the beat. I wasn't going to make it long, but I found myself writing a second verse, then a third verse, then a fourth and I was done. The Kiteman had to die at the end or it wouldn't be a real good story poem.

By highlighting the written products of our poetry project, I've run the risk of drawing attention to individual poems as if they were the most important feature that emerged from our immersion experience. That simply isn't so. The children's poetry allows the reader only a glimpse into the ways in which our community was transformed.

By far the most important feature to emerge from the weeks we spent immersed in poetry was the love of language that the children now carry with them. Not only did they develop the ability to listen for the voice of the text as both readers and writers but they discovered the pulse and power of the word within themselves.

References

Ryder, Joanne. 1985. *Inside Turtle's Shell and Other Poems of the Field.* New York: MacMillan Publishing Company.

Welty, Eudora. 1984. *One Writer's Beginnings.* Cambridge, MA: Harvard University Press.

THE SEASONS: A YEAR OF WRITING, ART, AND MUSIC

KATHERINE DOAK LINK
Diegueño Country School
Rancho Sante Fe, California

As a teacher, I am a basket collector. Long after I have consumed the homemade holiday cookies that my students pile high in baskets every year, I save the empty baskets. There is something about an empty basket that compels the imagination to fill it, perhaps with shells from a distant beach or with long-stemmed delphiniums from a future garden.

Some of the most useful gifts that I return to my students are empty baskets. Baskets in this sense refer to those general forms, constructs, or exercises that exist solely for students to fill with their writing. These baskets are idea-catchers, some of them tightly structured and others open and insubstantial as cirrus clouds. Many of the commonly used prewriting techniques—clustering, listing, brainstorming—are baskets; forms such as sonnets, haiku, and five-paragraph essays are baskets; archetypical constructs, such as the journey or trials of a heroine or hero are baskets.

I often remind myself that a basket is useful only as it inspires a child to fill it freely. When it has served its purpose as an idea-catcher, the written content naturally eclipses it. As Jacques Prevert suggests in his poem, "To Paint the Portrait of a Bird," once a writer has caught the metaphorical bird in a cage of written form, he or she may erase the surrounding bars. In other words, the structure that originally captured the idea—the basket or cage, if you will—must recede to a secondary position, allowing the content to sing like Prevert's bird.

In my experience as a writing teacher, I have found that most children benefit from being given nonrestrictive, empty baskets. Paradoxically, their freedom as writers is usually enhanced rather than diminished, especially if the construct is tangible enough to inspire confidence but flexible enough to stretch to the size of any memory or dream.

Last year, I used the broad construct of the passing seasons as a basket for my sixth-grade students to fill with writing, music, and art. Perhaps I unconsciously chose the theme of the seasons because, after three years of teaching in Southern California, I was hungry for the spectacular changes of leaf and cloud and snow that had structured my inner and outer life during fifteen years of living in Alaska. At any rate, I decided that one of the central sixth-grade writing projects of the year would be an individual book of poems by each child, based on the four seasons. Art and music wove their way into the basket almost effortlessly.

Summer

The heat of summer is still a tangible presence when the year begins at Diegueño Country School, a small private elementary school not far from San Diego. Once truly a country school, shaded by eucalyptus trees that the owners, Michael and Leah Cole, planted themselves, the school now shares the general neighborhood with a tennis resort, tract homes, and an occasional mansion. The building itself resembles an overgrown house, tumbling down a small hill like a boxy waterfall of additions, skylights, and wooden stairs. Inside, the kitchen of the original house serves as the office. The only administrative presence is an enormous wooden, rolltop desk with so many drawers that only Jennifer—the school secretary, tour guide, nurse, and diplomat—really knows how to locate the paper clips. During the three years that I have spent in the seven oddly shaped but airy classrooms, I have taught second, fourth, and sixth grade English and literature; fourth, fifth, and sixth grade music; and assorted electives, including astronomy, French, drama, and anthropology.

Last September began with poetry. My twenty-two sixth graders, whom I had taught when they were in fourth grade, were enthusiastic and sophisticated writers. For most of them, writing was as rewarding as kicking goals on the soccer field. After two months of vacation, summer was the first installment of our year long poetry book project. We proceeded leisurely about the process of writing the first pair of poems. First, we read and discussed poems about summer or about events that occurred in summer: "Heat" by H.D., "The Lake Isle of Innisfree" by William Butler Yeats, "The Fish" by Elizabeth Bishop, "On the Grasshopper and the Ant" by John Keats, "Summer Day" by Yuan Mei (translated by Kenneth Rexroth), a portion of "Knoxville: Summer of 1915" by James Agee, and "Watering the Garden," one of my own poems.

The children were delighted that I shared a summer poem of my own, especially since this one happened to have been published. I am convinced that exchanges of writing between students and teachers are most fruitful when they are two-way, when the teacher takes on the role of creator as well as facilitator. The children in my class had always enjoyed my memories, written and verbal, of life in a small cabin outside Fairbanks, Alaska. My home was situated on an old mining claim, and each year the spring run off flooded the sunken mine shafts with stagnant, amber water. The poem that I shared with my students concerned my daily trips to one of these abandoned shafts to fill buckets with water for my garden. The children were particularly struck by these lines about the old shaft: "its dark waters / scintillate with mosquito larvae / surfacing to breathe." "Scintillate" became the word of the season and cropped up in my students' poems all year. Justin Morris wrote:

> I'm sitting on scalding
> lava rock with a bamboo pole,
> waiting for a glamorous
> scintillating blue-finned tuna
> to yank my line and give me
> some action. . . .

One of my deepest pleasures as a teacher is to watch my students requisition some small part of what I have presented in class and wield it for their own ends, even if it is just a single word.

Often I am unaware of the impact of what has transpired in class until the effects surface in my students' writing and art. When we briefly interrupted our summer poems to design journal covers (which we mounted, laminated, and bound), I was surprised to see Megan Larmer's design. She had chosen her two favorite summer poems—Yuan Mei's "Summer" and H.D.'s "Heat"—and had copied them into the open book that she had drawn on her cover. The same flower petals that blow through the window in Yuan Mei's poem floated down from Megan's painted sky, obscuring some of the words of the poems.

We took the summer poems through a slow process of revision. After composing the initial raw drafts, the children reworked them for line breaks. Then, dividing into writing groups, they assisted each other in further revisions. They underlined in colored marker the lines and phrases that they particularly admired in each other's work and discussed the poems individually, taking the first few minutes of each session for nothing but praise. Then they asked questions for clarification, suggested places for expansion or improvement, and returned the poems to their group members, complete with generous written comments. Because many of the members of the class had journeyed together since kindergarten, they knew each other intimately and were well equipped to be honest and sensitive at the same time. Years of writing together had bonded them, and it was quite usual for close friends to dally in the classroom at lunchtime to read aloud their latest journal entries, essays, or stories. During writing group time, I merely floated from one group to another and submitted my own written comments along with the others.

While the children were coalescing the final drafts of their poems, we embarked on a freewriting project that I had concocted over the summer in Washington, D.C. For those of us who love art but cannot afford an original canvas, the National Gallery has a wealth of post cards. I chose them with my future sixth graders in mind: exquisite landscapes of the French countryside; portraits of intriguing characters; and action paintings of burning ships, snarling bears attacking hunters, and bloody battles. Dramatic content was one of my primary requirements. As I wandered through the museum, I was impressed by Thomas Cole's *The Voyage of Life*, a quartet of enormous paintings depicting the stages of human development. These, it turned out, were the most popular paintings of all among my students.

When I returned home with my post cards, I laminated them and taped them individually to a large bulletin board covered with vinyl. The children gently detached the post cards, returned to their seats to write about the masterpieces in their hands, and reattached them to the vinyl when they were done. Each student wrote several long freewrites, usually from the point of view of a character, object, or force in the painting. Of Thomas Cole's *Voyage of Life: Youth*, Lacie Weddle wrote:

As we sailed along the crystal rivers I stood there, arms streched out holding the golden hours of time. I am the most important creature in the world because I hold time, and if it weren't for me the world would probably be a whole lot worse because time is what makes people and animals age and things in the world change. One day my master sailed me through a secret passage of rainforest type greenery and out into the most beautiful river in the world. . . .

During freewriting, I always write with my students on the board, read aloud what I have written, and erase my words at the end of class. I am sometimes reminded of the Chinese poet Li Po, who is said to have written haunting poems, folded them into paper boats, and set them adrift on the river. Much of my own writing disappears in a similar way, dissolving into chalk dust because I opt to have my students observe me as I write. They've grown accustomed to my board scratchings and seem to share their work more readily because they have seen mine in process. My sixth graders were especially enthusiastic about sharing their art post card freewrites, and we discussed some of the artists and their work in conjunction with the students' imaginative conceptions.

It was well into autumn when the last drafts of the summer poems were finally complete. As a sample, here is one of Greg Hudson's poems in its entirety:

Dreaming the Mighty Deep

My fishing line
        is cast.
As it slices
        through the air,
I feel a warm tingle
        of hope
in my bones.
        I know I will catch a fish.
I will catch a fish
        as big as the sea,
with rainbows of color
        across its gleaming body.
I will cook it
        on a great grill
that stretches
        from Earth to Mars
where we will share
        our feast
before it spoils
        with the taste

of land air.

None shall starve

any longer.

I know I will catch a fish.

Fall

Unless you have cultivated an ornamental maple or a liquid amber tree in your yard, autumn can pass by all too invisibly in San Diego. I'm sure that local biologists could point to numerous subtle changes in the plant and animal kingdoms, but for someone who has relished the drama of fall in the northern woods, autumn in Southern California is disappointing. There are no golden pennants on the birches, no sharp smell of highbush cranberries along the paths, no deep satisfaction in accumulating cords of dry spruce.

Writing about autumn proved challenging for a few of my students, simply because they had never fully experienced it. As usual, we read and discussed a cluster of poems about autumn: "To Autumn" by John Keats, "Apparently with no surprise" by Emily Dickinson, "Autumn Rain" by Kenneth Rexroth, "Wind Tossed Dragons" by Hsieh Ngao (translated by Rexroth), and two Native American songs of thanksgiving, "The Lands Around My Dwelling" (Eskimo) and an Iroquois prayer. Then, for those who wanted visual images of fall, I distributed an assortment of old Audubon and Sierra Club desk calendars with their superb photographs of the seasons. While some students used these visual prompts, others brainstormed in pairs about their experiences during the fall.

After the children had written their first drafts, we talked extensively about line breaks. I showed them models of poems with short lines ("We Real Cool" by Gwendolyn Brooks), with long lines ("The Raven" by Edgar Allan Poe), with line breaks for word emphasis ("Sleeping in the Forest" by Mary Oliver), and with line breaks by phrase ("The Blessing" by James Wright). Then I handed out William Carlos Williams's poem "The Turtle," typed in paragraph form with no line breaks. The children devised their own line breaks for the poem, most of which were excellent, and finally, after sharing their various versions, read the poem as Williams published it. Surprisingly, this was one of the most satisfying poetry lessons of the year, for after this exercise, the children began to operate as line break artists in their own poems.

The final versions of their autumn poems reflected the means that each child used for gathering ideas, whether it be through a visual prompt, an exercise in imagery, or a personal memory. Becky Graul used a calendar photograph as the basis of her poem "Who":

> A mirror image of each other,
> Exact in every way,
> Two owls sit, their heads turned
> Toward each other,
> Their curious amber eyes absorbing
> The slowly changing
> Autumn surroundings. They perch
> In a spruce tree,
> On a dead branch
> That's covered in lichen
> And dangling gray beard moss. . . .

The visual, descriptive nature of her poem hints at the photograph she used for inspiration. Aaron Infante-Levy, on the other hand, chose to represent autumn in abstract, metaphorical terms. He simply searched for the best images:

> Autumn is . . .
> a pirate ship with no sails.
> It comes, bringing destruction and terror,
> leaving behind a frozen trail of red. . . .

Another student, Megan Larmer, wrote from her own personal experience, describing Thanksgiving at her home. She arranged a still life of the senses, complete with fine details: smells that "sift from the oven's tiny seams" and "glass peach goblets" and "burnished turkey" on the table. Then, in the middle of the poem:

> Some gangster in a movie
> coming from the television
> fills the genial atmosphere
> with a halting New York accent. . . .

Honest, well-crafted poetic surprises like this one remain in my memory for a long time. As a matter of fact, when the poetry project was finished at the end of the year, the children played a guessing game with me to see how much I remembered of their work. They were astonished that I could paraphrase or recite sections from most of the more than 166 poems. The explanation for this tour de force lay in their memorable writing rather than in my fallible memory.

Winter

In Alaska, the gradual return of the sun after the December solstice makes the bitter days of winter more bearable. I always celebrated when, in late January, the first slanted ray of direct sunlight illumined the cast iron frying pan hanging in my kitchen. My Southern California students knew winter as the end of rattlesnake season, as occasional frost on the soccer field, and, perhaps most of all, as midwinter travel to snowy places.

As we had done with the two previous seasons, we began our winter poems by reading. Some of my winter teaching favorites are "Winter" by William Shakespeare, "Those Winter Sundays" by Robert Hayden, "It sifts from Leaden Sieves—" by Emily Dickinson, "Velvet Shoes" by Elinor Wylie, and "The Terrace in the Snow" by Su Tung Po (translated by Rexroth). We paid special attention to imagery as we read these poems, and interesting winter images began cropping up in the children's poems. Samantha Childs wrote that "icicles hanging / from the trees are frozen candles / wax turned to ice. . . ." Later in the poem, they are lit by the distant stars. On a more mundane level, Raam Wong compared the winter smog to "a slovenly sock." Aaron Infante-Levy observed that snow "caresses me with disorganization. . . ," and Chris Michels ended a poem with the image of a howling wolf "making mist with his warm breath / as if his soul is being freed / from the prison of the body." One of my favorites is this stanza from David Mannix's poem:

> The chains on the Chevrolet are
> dying slaves, numb to the bone.
> They do tiresome somersaults endlessly
> on the white, teeth-chattering snow.

The images in these poems were born, in part, from a pact that we made as a class: We tried to eliminate what I call "grab bag language" from our work. As writers, most of us have our own personal grab bags, filled with stock poetic words and phrases. These are the words from which we think poetry is made before we start to look for more honest images. I sometimes set my students groaning by composing impromptu grab bag lines like these: "The delicate unicorn, its sapphire eyes / gleaming with love, soars tenderly / through the rainbow-strewn skies." Since I compose these saccharine lyrics myself, I can safely laugh at them without hurting anyone's feelings. I am convinced that when children reach a certain stage of confidence in their writing, it benefits them if we tactfully help them abandon their grab bags. While I encourage my students to show not tell, I also request honesty and fresh sight. The process is analogous to progressing beyond stick figure drawing; at last, uncomfortable though it may be at first, the artist must learn to represent more on paper that standardized images.

After several months of trying to write without grab bag words, the children became healthy critics of their own work. At the very end of the school year, as they typed their season poems, many of them looked askance at their old summer poems. Some of the lines written nine months earlier no longer reflected the children's finesse with language.

If time had allowed, I would have liked to have taken the winter poems one step further. The winter before, I held a midwinter song festival with my sixth-grade class, which, while it did not banish any arctic darkness, made the January return to school a little more palatable. My students that year were highly skilled readers, and we finished J.R.R. Tolkien's entire *Lord of the Rings* over the course of the year. Tolkien's epic is studded with songs that interrupt and elaborate on the narrative. So the children wrote their own tremendously varied songs: rap songs, hilariously reworded versions of standard tunes, and ballads set to original melodies. While some of the other students worked in pairs, Tamlin Pavelsky sat under a desk in the quietest corner of the room, composing a musical dialogue between a wanderer and a princess. He later sang it to me, and I wrote down the music and accompanied the song on my keyboard during the actual performance. A fragment of his ballad appears in Figure 1.

Another student, Anne Suskind, posed the question, "Oh ever wonder where cats are when they can't be found?" The stanzas of her song play off a series of geographical places that contain the word "cat":

> Well, some say they go to Egypt
> Where ancient cats were worshipped
> But I say they go to Catmandu,
> If I were a cat, then I would too.

In addition to composing lyrics like these for the festival, the children illustrated many of the episodes from *The Lord of the Rings* and displayed their drawings on the walls. Then, in true hobbit fashion, we ended our song festival with a feast that would have satisfied the appetite of even a Bilbo Baggins.

Figure 1

Performances such as these augment the many ways of publishing student writing and lend an air of festivity and importance to the children's work. Now that our school owns a fine assortment of Orff instruments, I plan to make them available to my students for future festivals. Perhaps we will even debut some of the children's original compositions at the concerts that we give several times a year for parents. Since I also happen to be the music teacher, that won't be difficult to arrange.

Spring

Spring, out of necessity, became the season for completing writing projects that had been germinating throughout the year. After reading novels of their choice, my sixth graders designed collage book covers, which we later laminated. On the sleeves, they wrote four distinct, typed blocks of prose: a paragraph to entice their friends to read the book, a portrait of the inner and outer qualities of the main character, a description of the setting, and a series of imaginative reviews of the book by fictitious critics. I have a personal bias against plot summaries, perhaps because of my teaching experience on the college level. Many of my college students found it difficult to break away from the habit of summarizing the plots of novels, plays, or stories when they wrote critical papers.

So now, teaching on the elementary level, I try to arrange book report assignments that circumvent the bloodhound approach of tracking the plot. On the back of her book cover, Monica Evans enticed her classmates with these words about *A Spell for Chameleon* by Piers Anthony:

> Xanth is a land of magic, filled with tangle trees, centaurs, and magic talents. All humans each have one original talent, such as curing feather fade in chickens, turning time backwards for five seconds, and other useless magic. Everyone, that is, except Bink. . . .

Paragraphs such as these were augmented by the children's book jacket illustrations, many of which captured the tone, theme, or setting of the individual novels.

At Diegueño Country School, spring is also the traditional time for Dig, an annual adventure in anthropology. The sixth graders and I elected to study the culture of Tibet. While I read aloud from a collection of excellent books about Tibet, they drew mandalas, fashioned masks based on the golden images of the Tibetan deities, and painted religious symbols on smooth rocks that I gathered from the beach. The highlight of our Dig experience was a visit by a Tibetan lama, Geshe Tsephel, who honored us by accepting our invitation to tell us about Tibetan religion, art, and history. After the Geshe had departed, Raam Wong wrote this poem about him:

> He is a waterfall
> of truth and love
>
> . . . .
> From war fields
> to forests,
> everyone is silent.
> There is peace—
> a stepped-on flower
> rises back up.

Raam included this poem in the spring section of his poetry book; not only had the Geshe visited during spring but his message had been one of resiliency despite the brutal political winter that lingers in his country.

As usual, reading spring poetry preceded writing about the last of our four seasons. There is an almost dizzying array of superb spring poems from which to choose: "Spring" by Thomas Nashe, "in Just-" by e. e. cummings, "Bee! I'm expecting you!" by Emily Dickinson, "Daffodils" by William Wordsworth, "Written on the Wall at Chang's Hermitage" by Tu Fu (translated by Rexroth), and "And When the Green Man Comes" by John Haines. Between reading poems, the children and I escaped from the classroom on nature walks, for spring suffuses the hills of Southern California with wild flowers and extraordinary shades of green. In one of his poems, Gabe Cole wrote about new crickets, "creaking like a thousand tiny doors." Joseph Bardin described the warming ocean, where "waves / crack like thorned / whips." Becky Graul observed that the ripples in a stream looked like "a sliced agate undulating."

Each child chose the finest from among his or her spring poems and transformed it into a Mother's Day gift (see Figure 2). For this project, I carted in my collection of ink stones, ink sticks, calligraphy brushes, models of Chinese characters, and stacks of absorbent newspaper. After the children had ground their own ink, practiced a little, and written the characters that appealed to them, they attached typed copies of their spring poems to the calligraphy sheets. We sped these through the copy machine onto ivory colored paper, trimmed them, and mounted the final products onto thick colored paper with folded borders of black at the tops and bottoms. When we attached loops of colored cord, the results were spectacular.

Then began the final assembly of our poetry books. While half of the class typed poems on the school computers, the other half drew illustrations. The children had been exposed to medieval illuminated texts in art class, and to illustrate their books, they illuminated the letters in large outlined words—"The Seasons" for each cover and "Summer," "Fall," "Winter," and "Spring" for pages to divide the sections of poetry. They took elaborate care as they drew miniature scenes and colorful designs inside their letters. This was the culmination of a year of work, and when the books were finally bound and returned to the authors, the children were immensely proud to present them to their parents.

Although I will almost certainly choose a different central project for next year's class, this year my sixth graders and I discovered that a basket of the seasons is easy to fill with rich examples of writing, art, and music. The only disadvantage to such a universal and flexible construct is that a multitude of unwritten poems, unsung songs, and invisible drawings are invariably left out of the basket. The year merely hinted at our potential.

Figure 2

Creek

Shala-Shaboom...
The river bank rushes by...
The imagination...
No limits...
The breeze blows...
The wollyragwort...
Like tormented prisoners...
I awaken to the...
Smell of fresh buttercups...
Of cinnamon and orange...
The banners snap...
Their individual thoughts...
Now one fortress of...
A spinning top...
A poppy!

Unfamiliar sound...
Distant and harsh...
The sound of a...
Bright yellow tractor...
Then one kind noise...
Glorious trees...
And the river...
Swaying to and fro like...
An old pendulum

AARON-INFANTE-LEVY

Fireworks!
Booming! Bursting! Flying! Floating!
Little parcels of flickering fire!
Like swarms of colored fireflies,
Soaring everywhere.
Fluorescent colors of neon light,
Shoelaces of squirming string,
Floating to the cooling earth.

They're like a child's
Finger painting,
With swirls of celestial color!
They are chaos,
In the form of light.
They look like the Milky Way
With assorted colors.

You will be mezmerized
By the hypnotic movement
Of the flying light
Like a snake
With swirling eyes!
Fireworks!

BYRON BINKLEY

WRITING CLASS AS MEDICINE WHEEL: PAUL'S STORY

MARGARET M. VOSS
University of New Hampshire
Durham, New Hampshire

W hen we ask children to tell the stories that matter to them, we invite them to reveal themselves, to express tough truths as well as everyday experiences. How do we create an environment where it's safe to be so honest? One answer is that we have to be brave enough to share ourselves and the stories that shape us. And we have to face unexpected issues and difficult truths with support, understanding, and respect. Here is a true story of one brave fourth-grade teacher and her students as I, a visiting researcher, witnessed it.

It's Friday, the end of the second week of school. Children have been writing "About the Author" pages about themselves to begin their individual "Best Books." These books will become collections of their polished pieces completed throughout the year. Today Betty Rea, the teacher, wants to begin choosing topics and writing in earnest. She has called everyone to the classroom library, also known as the "meeting area," a comfortable sunny space by the windows with a small, round table set before a couch and bookcases lined against the wall. The setting reminds me of a living room. There are a few regulation school chairs around the edges of the area, and children pull over some of the chairs from their desks, as well. A few sit on the floor. The group has formed a rough circle, and Betty begins. "We're gonna have storytelling," she says.

After referring to the oral tradition of a tale like *Jumping Mouse*, which she'd previously read to the children as part of their current unit on Native Americans, Betty continues, "Some of us will get to tell a story. Something that will interest us. I

suggest that you close your eyes and flip back through your life."
She closes her eyes. She leans ever so slightly forward with her
lips ever so slightly apart, attuned to her own memories. Then
Betty makes another link to the class' Native American study:
"This is the medicine wheel and these are truth stories." All is
quiet as each one thinks.

Finally Betty speaks again, offering to go first in the sharing.
"I thought of two stories—when I got my pony, Jitterbug, and
when my father died—one happy story and one sad story." She
asks which the children would like to hear and they vote. Sitting
on the sidelines, I know which I'd vote for and I suspect the
children will choose that one, too. I'm right. They want to know
about her father, though the voting margin is closer than I expect. I'm surprised that Betty has chosen such a serious topic at
the very beginning, and as I listen to her story, I'm doubly surprised, even as I admire her honesty and openness. Later she'll
tell me she didn't plan to tell this story. It just came to her, so in
her honesty she offered it. "If I'd thought about it, I might not
have told it," she'll later confide. Better that she hadn't thought
about it.

She begins:

> I grew up in East Texas. "That's the hump on the south side of
> Texas. My town was in the middle of that hump. My parents divorced
> when I was five.

Mei, sitting cross-legged on the rug in front of her teacher,
interjects in her soft voice, "That's sad." Betty agrees, "Yes, it's
sad, but I survived it; I'm here to tell it." She resumes her story.

> The court said, 'Ella, you get the kids during the school year. Peter,
> you get the kids in the summer.' My father lived on a farm, and we
> liked it there, but we missed our mother. When I was twelve and my
> brother was ten, my father left one morning. We kissed him good-
> bye and thought we'd see him at night. But he didn't come home
> that night. Someone came that night to say my father'd been killed.
> Later a man turned himself in; he'd shot him dead. He had an old
> grudge from when he lived on my father's farm. My father was a
> big, strong, handsome man—only 32, and the other man was small.
> Maybe my father had pushed him around, I don't know. But as I
> tell this story, it reminds me that if they'd talked it over when they
> were young, they probably would've worked it out and never had to
> resort to violence.

She pauses briefly, then adds, "This is one reason I don't like
violent stories."

The children are utterly silent, looking at their teacher and listening with total concentration. Betty asks for the children's stories, saying, "They don't have to be sad." No one moves. On the sidelines, I'm wondering if anyone will be brave enough to follow that story.

After several moments, Tyrone raises his hand. "When I lived in Georgia. . . ." he begins, and he goes on to tell how he and his friend made popguns using chinaberries and chased each other around the neighborhood. "It was very funny," he concludes. Betty explains to the children that chinaberries are hard, small berries. "Like a crabapple?" someone asks. "Yes, but smaller." She says Tyrone's story reminds her of a story about chinaberries that she wants to write about sometime, too.

All is quiet again, no volunteers. Until Paul raises his hand. "This is when my mother died."

I can feel the tension in the air, or maybe it's just in myself. I've heard teachers allude to Paul's past, and I know it's a tragic story, though no one seems to know what's truth and what's rumor. Paul's writing has already reflected a preoccupation with violence and death. Betty's story tapped something deep inside him; I'm surprised he's about to let it out. I can hardly breathe, and I wonder what the children are feeling. They're still and totally attentive.

Paul speaks directly, almost matter-of-factly.

> My mother was on drugs and stuff. She was a suicide. There are six of us kids. She told us to break all the plates. She told us to burn the coffee table. She told us to get out and do whatever we want. We ran out. Smoke was coming out. She was standing in the doorway; she could get out, but she didn't. She went back in and burned herself.

There's a long moment of silence. What can anyone say? A few children are looking at Paul, while others cast their eyes and heads down, maintaining some distance from this powerful revelation. I know it's important to say the right thing, and I can only feel glad I'm not Betty. I have no idea what I'd say, how I'd handle this with the right blend of sensitivity and acceptance. I'd like to put my arm around the child, but his body is stiff, his voice firm. My touch would be the wrong response, an intrusion.

Betty lets the silence lie. Just as I sense she's about to speak, a child says in a quiet voice, "Boy, Paul, you were really brave to tell that story."

I silently bless that child for the perfect response. Paul blurts out a little more about his sister being at a hospital in the city.

"For help," Betty says. "A healing place to get better."

He nods, and Betty comments, "That's very sad, a lot like my story. You seem very strong."

"It's nothing."

"You feel you've worked it out."

Then she says, "In the medicine wheel, you're a strong warrior, and you've worked it out. That's something Paul knows that's important in his life, and we respect him for telling it. We honor you, Paul, and the brave boy within who's told that story and worked very hard to get over that. Everybody goes through rough times. If you have hard stories in your life, you're not alone. If you're working it out, I honor you for that."

Lissa wipes her eyes, as I do. Betty waits, the children wait, then Betty asks if someone else has something to tell.

After a moment, someone offers a story about a targetshooting game at Disney World. Then they enlist me to tell a story from my childhood. They talk about writing the stories down. Betty says, "I like to think of writing as talking on paper." Then, meeting time over, a couple of the children hand out the writing folders as everyone moves back to their seats. I look at Betty across the dispersing circle of kids and our eyes lock briefly, amazed at what has just occurred.

Paul's story is seldom, if ever, referred to directly by the children again. But in the fire drill line later, I overhear Jemma, the toughest girl in the class, whisper hoarsely to Paul, "Did that really happen?" He nods. "I hate when that happens," Jemma confides, "when adults do things to their families. My grandfather. . . ."

And throughout the year, I marvel at the children's treatment of Paul. Even when they complain to him about his excessive wandering around the room or critique his stories for overly vivid violence, they don't put him down. They manage to be unsentimental yet sensitive. The tone was set at the beginning of the year. He's accepted as a brave warrior.

CALL FOR MANUSCRIPTS

W*orkshop* is an annual about the teaching of writing and reading. Each volume is centered around a theme and features articles by teacher-researchers of grades K-8, reports of firsthand observations that show a teacher in action and include the voices and writing of students and/or colleagues. Contributors are paid. The editors are currently soliciting submissions for the seventh volume.

Workshop 6 will be devoted to the theme **Teacher as Writer**. The notion that teachers of writing should be actively engaged in the process of writing is not new, but it is one that deserves more careful attention. Given the demands of our profession, is it possible to be both a teacher and a writer? Is it necessary? What happens in classrooms where teachers write for themselves as well as for their students? What compels teachers to publish their writing beyond the classroom? These are a few of the issues *Workshop 6* will explore.

Workshop 6: Teacher as Writer will also feature a wide range of poetry, fiction, and memoir by classroom teachers, some who are publishing their work for the first time. Due to the time constraints, as the editorship has changed, manuscripts for this volume have already been selected.

Workshop 7 will be devoted to the theme **What Do We Value?** With the nation's attention turning to the establishment of standards for all students, the question seems particularly relevant.

Students and teachers in schools across the country are discovering new and effective ways of evaluating language arts learning. Self-assessment has become a part of classroom life, as students demonstrate awareness of their own strengths and needs as learners. Three-way conferences invite parents to become partners with teachers and students, articulating what it is they value in their children's learning, both in and out of school. Portfolios—in all their shapes, sizes, and designs—enable students to reflect on their growth as readers, writers, speakers, and listeners and, in some cases, to integrate other disciplines into their language arts learning.

Workshop 7 will explore these and other developments in evaluation. We invite you to send manuscripts on a wide variety of topics on this theme. Here are a few possibilities, but do not limit yourself to these:

- How has the current research on evaluation affected classroom practice?
- How can evaluation be part of learning?
- Whose values count in the classroom—students', peers', teacher's, administrators', parents', community's, the English teaching profession's? Why? How is this manifested?
- How do we communicate what we value in reading, writing, speaking, and listening to our students? Are our evaluation systems explicit or mysterious?
- How do we make evaluation an ongoing process throughout the school year?
- In what ways do we honor multiple intelligences in our evaluation processes?
- In what ways do we honor cultural diversity in our evaluation processes?
- How do we handle the dual roles of teacher and evaluator?
- Can evaluation hinder learning? What can we do about that?
- How are teachers dealing with the plethora of standardized tests imposed by districts or states?
- What are some of the possibilities portfolios offer students, parents, and teachers?
- How have parent-teacher conferences changed to accommodate new evaluation policies?
- In what ways do we evaluate our own growth as teachers? As readers and writers?
- What new systems of evaluating faculty have proven useful to teachers?

The deadline for *Workshop 7: What Do We Value?* is February 15, 1994.

Manuscript Specifications for Workshop

When preparing a manuscript for submission to *Workshop*, please follow these guidelines:

- Contributors must be teachers of grades K-8, and submissions should be written in an active, first-person voice ("I").
- Contributions should reflect new thinking and/or practice, rather than replicate the published works of other teacher-researchers.
- Submissions must adhere to a length limit of 4,400 words per article (approximately 12½ pages typed double-spaced, including illustrations and references).
- *Everything* in the manuscript must be typed double-spaced, including block quotations and bibliographies.
- References should be cited according to the author-date system as outlined in *The Chicago Manual of Style*.
- Graphics accompanying manuscripts must be camera ready.
- Title pages should include address, phone numbers, and school affiliations.
- Manuscript pages should be numbered consecutively.
- Send two copies of the manuscript to one of the editors at the following addresses:

Linda Rief   Maureen E. Barbieri
23 Edgerly-Garrison Road   1030 Parkins Mill Road
Durham, NH 03824   Greenville, SC 29607

- Include a cover letter indicating for which volume of *Workshop* the manuscript is to be considered, as well as the contributor's school address, home address, home phone number, and grade level(s).
- Enclose a stamped, self-addressed manila envelope so the manuscript can be returned, either for revision or for submission elsewhere.
- If the manuscript is accepted for publication, the author will be required to secure written permission from each student whose work is excerpted.

This call for manuscripts may be photocopied for distribution to classroom teachers. The editors invite all interested teachers of grades K-8 to consider sharing discoveries about teaching and learning in the pages of *Workshop*.

ABOUT WORKSHOPS
1, 2, 3, AND 4

W*orkshop* is an annual written by and for teachers of grades K-8, a place for teachers to share their new practices and their students' responses. The contributors are experienced teacher-researchers who avoid gimmicks and prescriptions in order to focus on how students learn the language arts and what teachers can do to help. Each *Workshop* addresses a current topic in the teaching of reading and writing. Each volume also features a discussion between an expert teacher and a professional leader, an article by a writer of children's books, and an interview with another children's author.

Workshop 1

The theme of *Workshop 1* is Writing and Literature. Its authors examine what is possible when teachers who understand real reading and writing bring them together so that students can engage in and enjoy both, draw naturally and purposefully on their knowledge of both, and discover what the authors and readers of a variety of genres actually do. A wealth of children's literature plays an essential role in their K-8 classrooms.

Readers will learn exciting new approaches to the teaching of writing and reading from teachers who understand both processes from the inside.

Contents: About *Workshop 1 Nancie Atwell* Seeking Diversity: Reading and Writing from the Middle to the Edge *Linda Rief* Casey and Vera B. *Barbara Q. Faust* An Author's Perspective:

Letters from Readers *Ann M. Martin* P. S. My Real Name Is Kirstin *Daniel Meier* The Teacher Interview: Jack Wilde *An Interview by Thomas Newkirk* When Literature and Writing Meet *Donna Skolnick* A Garden of Poets *Cora Five* Everyday Poets: Recognizing Poetry in Prose *Marna Bunce* From Personal Narrative to Fiction *Kathleen A. Moore* Historical Fiction: The Tie That Binds Reading, Writing, and Social Studies *Patricia E. Greeley* We Built a Wall *Carol S. Avery* Fossil Hunters: Relating Reading, Writing, and Science *Rena Quiroz Moore* The Author Interview: Carol and Donald Carrick *An Interview by Mary Ellen Giacobbe* One of Us *Carol J. Brennan* Process and Empowerment *Karen Weinhold*

Workshop 2

The theme of *Workshop 2* is Beyond the Basal. Although there is a definite movement toward new approaches to teaching reading, basal series are still dominant, and teachers who venture beyond them are in the minority. This book is directed to teachers who want to implement a literature-based curriculum and have questions about organizing a classroom that is not dependent on the structure created by a basal program.

The contributors to *Workshop 2* are teachers who have found practical, rewarding, and effective ways to move beyond basals and to make literature, students' responses to literature, and their own knowledge the heart of reading instruction. Readers, regardless of their experience, will be encouraged to bring literature into their students' lives.

Contents: About *Workshop 2 Nancie Atwell* Stephen and *The Haunted House:* A Love Story *Barbara Q. Faust* An Author's Perspective: The Room in Which Van Gogh Lived *Cynthia Rylant* Nebuchadnezzar Meets Dick and Jane: A Reader's Memoir *Ginny Seabrook* The Silences Between the Leaves *Marni Schwartz* Responding to the Call *Kathy Matthews* Once upon a Time in Room Seven *Kathleen A. Moore* The Author Interview: Jack Prelutsky *An Interview by Kathy Hershey* Audience: Key to Writing About Reading *Cyrene Wells* Talk: Responding to Books the Collaborative Way *Adele Fiderer* The Teacher Interview: Carol Avery *An Interview by Jane Hansen* Children as Authorities on Their Own Reading *Bobbi Fisher* Writing and Reading Literature in a Second Language *Dorothy M. Taylor* Beyond Labels: Toward a Reading Program for All Students *Joan Levy and Rena Moore* Apprenticeship: At Four or Fourteen *Linda Rief*

Workshop 3

The theme of *Workshop 3* is The Politics of Process. The authors describe the efforts of teachers and administrators who have engaged in the politics of process in order to teach writing and reading as they believe they should. They have joined forces with like-minded colleagues, invited dialogue with administrators, created opportunities for parents to see their children's school experience with new eyes, developed appropriate methods of evaluating literacy, and made the community part of their responsibility as teachers.

This volume is a practical invitation to teachers and administrators who are seeking strategies that will help them gain acceptance for process approaches to writing and reading in their schools.

Contents: About *Workshop 3 Nancie Atwell* An Invitation to Bake Bread *Linda Hazard Hughs* A Letter to Parents About Invented Spelling *Mary Ellen Giacobbe* An Author's Perspective: The Koala as a Teacher of Reading *Mem Fox* Portfolios Across the Curriculum *Mark Milliken* Evaluation: What's Really Going On? *Lynn Parsons* A Guest Essay: The Middle Class and the Problem of Pleasure *Thomas Newkirk* Setting the Stage *Mimi DeRose* The Teacher Interview: Toby Kahn Curry and Debra Goodman *An Interview by Yetta Goodman with Commentary by Ken Goodman* The Sun Does Not Set in Ganado: Building Bridges to Literacy on the Navajo Reservation *Sigmund A. Boloz* A Guest Essay: Learning Literacy Lessons *Patrick Shannon* "Change the Word Screw on Page 42" *Ed Kenney* Publishing and the Risk of Failure *Marguerite Graham* The Author Interview: Bill Martin, Jr. *An Interview by Ralph Fletcher* On Becoming an Exemplary Teacher: Having Dinner with Carol *Margaret Lally Queenan.*

Workshop 4

The latest volume in the series, *Workshop 4* explores the issue of teacher research in the language arts.

Contributors examine topics like writing development, collaboration in the classroom, self-assessment, and extending the range of student writing. Several authors investigate in their essays the ways teachers describe their classrooms, both what teachers include in their stories and what they omit.

Contributors to this volume of *Workshop* include Regie Routman, author of *Transitions* and *Invitations*, fiction writer Jean

Craighead George, author/illustrator Barbara Cooney, and Donald Murray, contributing an essay on poetry as a way of knowing.

Contents: About *Workshop 4 Thomas Newkirk Research as Storytelling:* Teacher-Researcher-Storyteller, *T. Gillespie* Silences in Our Teaching Stories—What Do We Leave Out and Why?, *T. Newkirk* The Ethics of Our Work in Teacher-research, *P. Johnson. Research as Reflection and Observation:* In Regie's Garden: An Interview with Regie Routman, *M. Barbieri* Curiosity in the Classroom, *B. Gravelle* Dreaming Away: Adventures in Non-Fiction, *T. Hillmer* Neverending Exposition, S. Raivio Ask Them, *K. Moore* "This Fish Is So Strange To Me": The Use of the Science Journal, *B. Rynerson. Research as Collaboration and Coteaching:* Academic Learning and Bonding: The Three-Year Classroom, *V. Swartz* Partnership in Process: Strengthening the Teacher-Learner-School Triangle, *R. Levi & G. Wood* Children Helping Children: A Cross-Grade Reading and Writing Program for Chapter 1 Students, *S. Haertel. Research as Art—Art as Resarch:* Author Interview: Jean Craighead George, *L. Lenz* - Daffodils in Manhattan, *K. Ernst* How Poems Think, *D. Murray-* Author Interview: *Barbara Cooney, S. Stires.*